The Silk Road in World History

The New
Oxford
World
History

The Silk Road in World History

Xinru Liu

OXFORD
UNIVERSITY PRESS

2010

OXFORD
UNIVERSITY PRESS

Oxford University Press, Inc., publishes works that further
Oxford University's objective of excellence
in research, scholarship, and education.

Oxford   New York
Auckland   Cape Town   Dar es Salaam   Hong Kong   Karachi
Kuala Lumpur   Madrid   Melbourne   Mexico City   Nairobi
New Delhi   Shanghai   Taipei   Toronto

With offices in
Argentina   Austria   Brazil   Chile   Czech Republic   France   Greece
Guatemala   Hungary   Italy   Japan   Poland   Portugal   Singapore
South Korea   Switzerland   Thailand   Turkey   Ukraine   Vietnam

Published by Oxford University Press, Inc.
198 Madison Avenue, New York, NY 10016

www.oup.com

Oxford is a registered trademark of Oxford University Press

Library of Congress Cataloging-in-Publication Data
Liu, Xinru.
The Silk Road in world history / Xinru Liu.
p. cm.
ISBN 978-0-19-516174-8; ISBN 978-0-19-533810-2 (pbk.)
1. Silk Road—History.
2. Silk Road—Civilization.
3. Eurasia—Commerce—History.
4. Trade routes—Eurasia—History.
5. Cultural relations. I. Title.
DS33.1.L58 2010
950.1—dc22
2009051139

11 13 15 17 19 18 16 14 12 10

Printed in the United States of America
on acid-free paper

*Frontispiece: In the golden days of the Silk Road, members of the elite in China
were buried with ceramic camels for carrying goods across the desert, hoping to enjoy
luxuries from afar even in the other world.* © Victoria and Albert Museum, London

For Weiye and Yafeng, scientists who also understand history

Contents

Editors' Preface

This book is part of the New Oxford World History, an innovative series that offers readers an informed, lively, and up-to-date history of the world and its people that represents a significant change from the "old" world history. Only a few years ago, world history generally amounted to a history of the West—Europe and the United States—with small amounts of information from the rest of the world. Some versions of the "old" world history drew attention to every part of the world *except* Europe and the United States. Readers of that kind of world history could get the impression that somehow the rest of the world was made up of exotic people who had strange customs and spoke difficult languages. Still another kind of "old" world history presented the story of areas or peoples of the world by focusing primarily on the achievements of great civilizations. One learned of great buildings, influential world religions, and mighty rulers but little of ordinary people or more general economic and social patterns. Interactions among the world's peoples were often told from only one perspective.

This series tells world history differently. First, it is comprehensive, covering all countries and regions of the world and investigating the total human experience—even those of so-called peoples without histories living far from the great civilizations. "New" world historians thus share in common an interest in all of human history, even going back millions of years before there were written human records. A few "new" world histories even extend their focus to the entire universe, a "big history" perspective that dramatically shifts the beginning of the story back to the big bang. Some see the "new" global framework of world history today as viewing the world from the vantage point of the Moon, as one scholar put it. We agree. But we also want to take a close-up view, analyzing and reconstructing the significant experiences of all of humanity.

This is not to say that everything that has happened everywhere and in all time periods can be recovered or is worth knowing, but that there is much to be gained by considering both the separate and interrelated stories of different societies and cultures. Making these connections is still another crucial ingredient of the "new" world history. It emphasizes connectedness and interactions of all kinds—cultural, economic, political, religious, and social—involving peoples, places, and processes. It makes comparisons and finds similarities. Emphasizing both the comparisons and interactions is critical to developing a global framework that can deepen and broaden historical understanding, whether the focus is on a specific country or region or on the whole world.

The rise of the new world history as a discipline comes at an opportune time. The interest in world history in schools and among the general public is vast. We travel to one another's nations, converse and work with people around the world, and are changed by global events. War and peace affect populations worldwide as do economic conditions and the state of our environment, communications, and health and medicine. The New Oxford World History presents local histories in a global context and gives an overview of world events seen through the eyes of ordinary people. This combination of the local and the global further defines the new world history. Understanding the workings of global and local conditions in the past gives us tools for examining our own world and for envisioning the interconnected future that is in the making.

Bonnie G. Smith
Anand Yang

The Silk Road in World History

CHAPTER I

China Looks West

From the time Eurasians started using polished stone tools to plant and harvest crops and to keep domesticated animals, they began to split into two distinct societies divided by the Tianshan, Altai, and Caucasus mountain ranges. To the fertile south, people became farmers. But on the Eurasian steppe, people continued to herd livestock such as cattle, sheep, and horses. Their herds fed in the cool mountains in summer, where the grass was lush, and were shepherded in winter to warmer valleys and plains. Each group of nomads grazed its animals according to a fixed annual pattern. However, climate changes and political conflicts with other nomads or with agricultural societies to the south often forced nomads out of their normal rounds. The movements of nomadic populations and their livestock continually threatened the settled lives of farmers, whose crops could be quickly destroyed by herds. Sometimes these displaced people and their herds moved westward in search of more fertile grasslands in western Asia and eastern Europe.

Some time around 600 BCE, horseback riding had begun to spread on the Eurasian steppe, and by the 400s BCE, nomads on the north border of the agricultural zone had learned to combine horsemanship with archery to become masters of the horse as a military machine. It is about this time, when these cavalries emerged, that our story of organized trade and communication along the steppe thoroughfares begins, for it was nomads on the Central Asian steppe who brought West and East together.

In the fifth century BCE, seven agricultural states in what is now eastern China were fighting each other for supremacy. In addition to fighting with each other, three northern states, the Qin, Zhao, and Yan, also had to cope with frequent incursions of nomadic cavalry.

Nomads from the steppe raided villages and towns, looting millet and wheat, the major grains of north China, and silks, which were common in China but considered rare and precious among nomads on the western steppe. Sericulture, the process of raising silk worms and extracting silk yarn, had appeared in China in the third millennium BCE; Zhou Dynasty folk songs of the early first millennium BCE frequently refer to silk weaving and textiles.

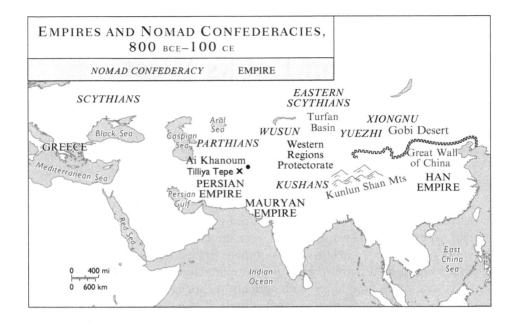

EMPIRES AND NOMAD CONFEDERACIES,
800 BCE–100 CE

NOMAD CONFEDERACY   EMPIRE

The mounted archers of the steppe had the advantage of speed and surprise. In an effort to defend themselves, the three northern states built walls along the mountain ranges to divide the agricultural and pastoral zones. Realizing the advantage of the nomads' tactics and horsemanship, the state of Zhao, under King Wuling, reformed its army in the fourth century BCE. His troops began to master the bow and arrow and began to dress in trousers and tight-sleeved robes as the nomads did. The members of his court heaped criticism on these reforms, since they considered the nomads "barbarians" and unworthy of any emulation. Prince Cheng, the king's uncle and an important courtier, advised:

> wise and intelligent people reside and all material wealth gathers
> here; sages and saints teach here, good morals dominate here,
> poetry, prose, rituals, and music are practiced here, and efficient
> technological inventions are tested here. People of faraway countries
> admire and learn from here, barbarians emulate the ways things
> are done here. Now your majesty is giving up our high standards to
> follow the clothing style of outsiders, thereby changing the teachings
> of our ancestors and the ancient ways. This will upset your people
> and make scholars angry, as it deviates from the values of the Middle

Kingdom [China]. Your majesty's subject wishes you to reconsider your decision.[1]

Nevertheless, the Zhao state's adoption of its enemies' military practices continued and improved its defenses.[2] Once the superiority of nomadic tactics and weaponry to the traditional horse and chariots and infantry was demonstrated, other northern Chinese states followed Zhao's example.

Such reforms increased the need for horses. The agricultural societies did not have the knowledge or the pasture to produce good horses, especially military mounts. Only the vast grassland could breed large numbers of fast, hardy horses with great endurance. Obtaining such horses was not easy. During the third century BCE, the Yuezhi, who lived in a region relatively near China, northwest of its western borders, between the northern foothills of the eastern end of the Tianshan Mountains and the Turfan Depression, had emerged as a powerful confederacy on the steppe. They maintained a friendly trading relationship with agricultural China. The minister and economist Guanzi (?–645 BCE) in his treatise on the economics of the Qi state argued that jade supplied by the Yuezhi should be the most highly valued currency of the state. "Our ancestor kings attributed the highest value to jade, as it came from a long distance. Gold is the second, and copper currency is the third."[3]

From antiquity, Chinese societies of the Yellow River Valley and the Yangzi River Valley had treasured jade more than gold. Most of the jade items found in their rulers' tombs were made of materials from Khotan, an oasis on the southern edge of the Takla Makan Desert in modern Xinjiang. The Yuezhi had been middlemen between China and Central Asia in ancient times. During the Warring States period, when the northern Chinese desperately needed good horses to supply their cavalries, they naturally turned to the Yuezhi.

East of the Yuezhi territory, on the Mongolian grassland, lived the Xiongnu, another powerful nomadic confederacy. Unlike the Yuezhi, they were in constant conflict with nearby Chinese states. When the first emperor of the Qin Dynasty, indeed the first emperor of China, Shihuangdi—which means simply "first emperor"—united the seven warring states and established the Qin Empire in 221 BCE, the Xiongnu were the foremost threat to his imperial power. The Qin, and later Han, rulers sent large quantities of silk textiles and floss (a silk padding used to make quilted cloth for the cold winter on the steppe) to appease the nomads or to trade for horses. Some of the silks were government-made products for presentation to the Xiongnu nobles, but many more were plain silk textiles produced by farm women. Silk textiles were used to line fur coats, and silk floss was used to pad quilted cloths. The quilted cloth was not only warm but also extremely light, and it was used not only for bedding but was also made into jackets and trousers. Such exquisite silk garments made the chieftains on the steppe look much more elegant than their followers. In this early international commerce, it was largely the ruling elites, whether nomadic or sedentary, and their demand for exotic goods from foreign lands, not the urge to market their own products, that motivated the trade. Only rare and luxurious goods from far away could mark the difference between the ruling elite and their subjects. The principal reason the chief of the Xiongnu nomads distributed Han silk robes was to demonstrate the political hierarchy of his confederacy and maintain the loyalty of his most important followers. Silk became the symbol of power and prestige on the steppe.

In addition to silk diplomacy, the Qin emperor fended off the constant Xiongnu raids by linking the walls previously built by different states to form the Great Wall, which ran all along the border between agricultural China and the steppe. To build the wall, he used peasants and convicts. Where there were gates in the wall, markets formed where farmers and herdsmen exchanged their products. Among the nomads who came to trade, one chief of the Yuezhi, whose surname was Luo, made a fortune selling good horses to the Chinese. The horses of the Tianshan foothills were taller and stronger than those of the Xiongnu, and Luo sold many of them to Shihuangdi for silks, which he then sold to other chiefs on the steppe. The chiefs paid him, according to the historian Sima Qian of the second century BCE, "ten times his original investment with their livestock." This wealth probably made the nomad Luo not only rich but also powerful among his followers. "The first emperor of the Qin showed his appreciation by granting Luo a position of the same rank as the highest ministers in the court," according to Sima Qian.[4] The Yuezhi became the great ally of the Qin Empire by supplying them with crucial military mounts.

The Qin Dynasty (221–207 BCE) ruled with strict and cruel laws and exhausted its people with many large projects, including the Great Wall, which caused unrest in the country. It was soon replaced by the Han Dynasty (206 BCE–220 CE), whose rulers also faced a persistent threat from the Xiongnu on its northern borders. The early Han Empire had just emerged from a devastating civil war, which had ended the Qin Dynasty, and was in a completely defensive position. The Xiongnu once surrounded the Han's founding emperor, Gaozu, on the northern frontier of the empire and almost took him prisoner. Many lands were laid waste, and horses were in short supply. Even ministers lacked horses and had to ride on bull carts in royal processions, and the emperor could not afford the full majestic chariot of four horses.

Gaozu and the next few emperors resorted to diplomacy to appease the Xiongnu. They sent princesses of the Han court, some genuine, some not, to the *shanyu* (chief) of the Xiongnu, to become his brides. The Han court hoped that in the future the shanyu might be the son of a Han princess, and friendlier toward the Chinese. The princesses brought with them large dowries, mostly silks and food grains, and the Xiongnu chiefs in turn presented horses as gifts to their new fathers-in-law. We do not know whether there ever was a shanyu at this time whose mother was a Han princess. Even if there had been one, it is hard to imagine that he would have improved the nomads' attitude toward the Chinese. But the exchange of gifts, including Chinese royal brides, ensured periodic peace and trade around the gates of the Great Wall.

After more than sixty years of recovery, the Han Empire gained enough strength to stop sending its princesses to the nomads, ending what the founding emperors had regarded as a humiliating practice. But the concept remained as a diplomatic tool. A century later, when the Xiongnu confederacy had split into northern and southern factions, the shanyu of the Southern Xiongnu, Huhanxie, asked for the hand of a Han princess by way of making a Han alliance against the northerners. The Han emperor, Yuandi, took this opportunity to make peace with the southern Xiongnu and enjoined his courtiers to select a beauty from his outer harem, the residence of the many beautiful girls sent to the court from various parts of the empire to wait for their chance to be chosen by the emperor as the favorite one. Most women spent their whole lives there without ever seeing the emperor. The "lucky" ones might "accompany the emperor to his tomb." The beautiful and accomplished Wang Zhaojun, because of her hopeless and bleak existence there, volunteered for the harsh life on the steppe. Yuandi, seeing her for the first time on the day of the ceremony at which she was presented to Huhanxie, was stunned by her great beauty and wanted to keep her in his palace. Nevertheless, the marriage alliance was deemed too strategically important to be called off and proceeded as planned.

It turned out to be quite beneficial for both sides. The presence of Wang Zhaojun at the Xiongnu court ensured frequent exchanges of gifts and greetings between the steppe and the Han Empire. She gave birth to several princes and princesses who were inclined toward friendship with the Han. Despite difficulties caused by domestic problems on both sides, a peaceful relationship between the two regimes lasted for several decades. Zhaojun missed her native Chinese culture, especially because she was a talented musician accustomed to the elegance of the Han court. In remembrance of her bravery and dedication, the Chinese people named several places after her and built temples in her honor to mark her route into the steppe. Many folk stories, paintings, musical works, and dramas have depicted her beauty, her musical talent, her sorrow about leaving her homeland, and her loneliness living in a foreign land. The story of Wang Zhaojun became one of the most popular themes of literature and art along the Silk Road.

She was only one of the Han princesses who married nomad chiefs and carried dowries of Chinese culture to the steppe. While such intermarriages brought temporary periods of peace on the border, the nomads and the Chinese continued to war and trade for many centuries, in spite of the rise and fall of various powers on the steppe and of different regimes in agricultural China.

A capable Chinese emperor, Wudi, took the offensive against the Xiongnu soon after he ascended the throne in 140 BCE. He sent military expeditions to the steppe and captured numerous herds of horses and sheep, while pushing the nomads away from the Chinese borders. However, the Xiongnu, as a migratory people, never considered a retreat a defeat, and they never intended to conquer and rule the agricultural lands. They continued to loot Chinese villages and towns. The emperor Wudi still desperately needed allies among nomadic warriors to ensure peace along the borders of his empire.

When news of conflict between the Yuezhi and the Xiongnu reached the Han court early in the reign of Wudi, he decided to send an envoy westward to the Yuezhi, hoping to make an alliance with them against the Xiongnu. No dignitary was willing to undertake the dangerous journey into this region unknown to the Chinese, but a petty official named Zhang Qian answered the call. He set off for the west with a hundred followers, including a native of the steppe, Ganfu. The only known route to the west passed through the territory of the Xiongnu, who detained Zhang Qian and his men. He had no choice but to stay with the Xiongnu imperial camp, a delay that cost him a decade. He spent ten years moving with them on the steppe, during which time he married a Xiongnu woman and fathered her children. Nevertheless, he kept the emblem of his office as envoy of the Han emperor throughout his captivity and eventually managed to escape the Xiongnu camp and reach the territory of Dawan (modern Ferghana in Uzbekistan). The king of Dawan escorted him south to Kangju, or Sogdiana, also in modern Uzbekistan, and from there he reached the court of the Yuezhi on the bank of the Oxus River in 129 BCE.

Around 130 BCE, the Xiongnu had defeated the Yuezhi, traditional allies of the Chinese. The number of horseback-riding archers a confederacy could muster was the measure of its strength, and the Xiongnu confederacy could claim about 300,000 cavalrymen, the entire adult male population.[5] In triumph, the chief of the Xiongnu had killed the leader of the Yuezhi and had his skull made into a drinking vessel, a symbol of victory on the steppe. The Yuezhi, defeated and humiliated, left their homeland in what is now Xinjiang Province and migrated across the pastures north of the Tianshan range all the way to Bactria. Along the way, some branches of the Yuezhi left the main group and settled at the eastern end of the Tianshan range. Another group also splintered off and stayed along the route through Ferghana in present-day Uzbekistan. The main contingent, however, with a military strength of 100,000–200,000 horse archers, arrived at the north bank of the Amu Darya, as it is known today (the Greeks had called this river the Oxus). Some two hundred years earlier, this area had been a Greek colony established during the eastern expedition of Alexander the Great in the fourth century BCE, and the Greeks had called it Bactria. Stretching from what today is the northern part of Afghanistan to Uzbekistan, Bactria was a fertile agricultural land, dotted with Hellenistic cities.

When Zhang Qian arrived, the Yuezhi chief, with his father's killing at the hands of the Xiongnu fresh in his mind, had no interest in a military alliance with the Han against them. He was happily settled in Bactria and had no wish to go back to the steppe to face the Xiongnu again. Although Zhang Qian spent more than a year in the Yuezhi court, he was unable to persuade their chief to change his mind. On his way back to China, Zhang Qian was captured by the Xiongnu again. However, this time he managed to get away from them much sooner; just a year later, the death of the shanyu and the civil war that followed provided him with an opportunity to escape. He returned with his Xiongnu wife and children and the loyal Ganfu to the Han court in the city of Chang'an.[6]

Zhang Qian reported all the details of his thirteen-year journey to the "Western Regions" to the emperor Wudi. His original reports no longer exist, but both Sima Qian's *History* and the official *History of the Han* preserve large portions of it. Although Zhang Qian failed to carry out his political mission, his report opened the eyes of the emperor and his courtiers. Prior to Zhang Qian's journey, the so-called Western

Regions had been little more than a mythic land mentioned in ancient Chinese legends. Having spent eleven years following the movement of the Xiongnu camp, Zhang Qian had not only became familiar with the mountains, deserts, and routes of the steppe but also learned much about the customs and political structure of the Xiongnu and other nomadic peoples. Virtually all knowledge about these early nomads on the eastern steppe comes from Zhang Qian's report. Excavations of tombs presumably belonging to Xiongnu chiefs of this period in Mongolia have revealed information largely in agreement with his observations about these nomads' lives. In addition to the information he provides regarding other nomadic and agricultural-pastoral societies in Central Asia, he tells about the Parthians who lived on the Iranian Plateau. This people, whose country he called Anxi, made exquisite silver coins engraved with the face of their king, a novel practice to Chinese emperors. Zhang Qian also refers vaguely to countries further west, including those on the shores of the eastern Mediterranean, one of which he calls Tiaozhi, probably a transliteration of Antioch. His report also contains information about the migrations of the Yuezhi, who were willing to resume contacts with the Han court.

During his stay in Bactria, Zhang Qian had noticed that a specific kind of bamboo and cloth from southwest China's Shu region was selling well in the markets of Bactria. This bit of information was very interesting to him and the Han court. When he asked the Bactrian traders where they had acquired these goods, they answered: India.[7] He did not go to India himself, but he gives a fairly accurate account of it, including its tropical climate and its use of war elephants. Presumably, he had gathered this information in Bactrian marketplaces. His report about all the exotic goods he had seen, such as the large, beautiful horses of Central Asia and glassware from even further west, and the existence of international trade goods made in a southwestern region of China, impressed the emperor Wudi very much. But the only known routes to these luxuries lay through the steppe, still under Xiongnu control.

Zhang Qian had been very lucky to escape twice from Xiongnu captivity, and he was not anxious to enter their territory again. On the basis of the bamboo and cloth he had seen in Bactria, he thought that there must be an alternate route to the west. If those southwestern Chinese goods had reached Bactria from India, there had to be a more direct route connecting India and China. He suggested to Wudi that he send expeditions to explore other ways to get to India that circumvented the Xiongnu. Wudi took his advice and did so, but without success. In order to get from Sichuan to India, the only possible land route was to cut through the mountainous regions of Yunnan, which was then outside the bounds of China. People living in that area saw no benefit to themselves from any encroachment of Han trade routes into their territory. They resisted or killed any intruders. As a result, dangerous though it might be, the steppe route remained the most viable thoroughfare to Central Asia and parts further west.

Meanwhile, the Han campaign against the Xiongnu outside the Great Wall continued. After several successful military expeditions sent onto the steppe by Wudi, the Xiongnu were no longer a direct threat to the farmers along the north borders of China. The interests of both sides shifted to trade and protecting trade routes. To secure China's access to the routes to the Western Regions, Wudi had to protect the long corridor between part of the Tibetan plateau and the Mongolian desert from Xiongnu raids. Wudi had the Great Wall extended northwestward all

Zhang Jun, a cavalry commander for the Eastern Han Dynasty (25–220 CE), was buried with this chariot, along with an array of sculptures of mounted soldiers, in Wuwei, China. The chariot symbolized Zhang Jun's status in life. Cavalry presence increased in Han military forces during their prolonged war with the Xiongnu along the Great Wall and on the steppe. Erich Lessing / Art Resource, NY

the way to the Gate of Jade (Yumen), the westernmost garrison town, near Dunhuang. He then set up a system of garrisons all along this part of the Great Wall and put its headquarters in a town called Anxi ("Tranquil West").

This relatively safe route drew many foreign merchants to the gates of the Great Wall. More and more exotic goods—Roman glassware, Indian cotton textiles, spices and fragrances, gemstones, and woolen textiles of various origins—arrived in the capital city of Chang'an via the Gate of Jade. In addition to the goods, information on foreign climates, foods, clothing, and currencies came over this route, and Chinese historians began to accumulate details about places as far away as South Asia and the Mediterranean.

Chinese rulers also started to realize the international value of silk textiles, which were so common at home that every farming household paid a tax to the Han government in grain and silk cloth. Men tilled the land and women raised mulberry trees, using the leaves to feed silk worms. They extracted silk fiber from the cocoons, spun silk yarn, and wove silk textiles. Exquisite textiles such as brocade, tapestry, and embroidered silk cloth, which demanded complicated looms, high technical skill, and a sophisticated division of labor, were mainly the products of large workshops under government control.

The trade in silk with the nomads spread the fame of these Chinese textiles beyond the steppe. In Zhang Qian's later career as ambassador to the Wusun, a nomadic group roaming to the west of the Xiongnu, he and his three hundred envoys with six hundred horses carried "tens of thousands of cattle and sheep, gold and silk worth millions" to ensure an alliance.[8] Since most societies knew how to make textiles only from animal fur or plants, the idea of producing silk cloth from a worm seemed miraculous to them. With the migration of the Yuezhi to Bactria, the unique cloth naturally followed them westward. Although military conflicts among the Xiongnu, the Yuezhi, and the Han Empire sometimes disrupted transportation, they also contributed to the demand for certain trade goods on this route, which soon became one of the major communication and transportation arteries of Eurasia that, taken together, came to be known in modern times as the Silk Road. The Silk Road was a system of commercial routes, on both land and sea, that linked various peoples from China to the Mediterranean.

New communities of traders settled along these routes to meet the demand for luxury goods at either end of this route system. The merchants often organized themselves into caravans—trading teams that carried goods on pack animals or carts. To host the caravans, beginning around the early first century BCE during the reign of the Han emperor Wudi, caravan cities started to form along the trunk routes of the Silk Road. Since the Han court took great interest in the goods coming from the west, guaranteeing their safety was high on the agenda of this powerful emperor. Traveling along the steppe routes on horseback was fast but not safe, as Zhang Qian had learned by being twice detained by the Xiongnu. As mentioned, during the early Han Dynasty's offensive campaigns against the Xiongnu, Wudi had extended the Great Wall as far as the Gate of Jade in order to protect a newly established trade route, the Hexi Corridor (through modern Gansu Province). Literally "the corridor departing from the west bank of the Yellow River," this long strip of relatively flat land was flanked by the Qilian Mountains on its southern side and the Mongolian deserts along its northern side. Wherever water flowed down from the mountaintops, oases had formed between the mountains and the sandy bottom of Talim Basin, and it was possible to grow crops in these scattered locations. However, since the oases were surrounded by sandy deserts, maintaining a sustainable agriculture required a constant struggle against threatening sand dunes. To stabilize the dunes and maintain irrigation channels would require a large investment of time and resources in planting vegetation.

Routes passing through deserts and oases are better suited for camels than for horses. The Hexi Corridor was one of the domains of Central Asia's domesticated two-humped camel (also known as the Bactrian camel to distinguish it from the one-humped Arabian camel). The camels' humps store fat that helps them survive travel through the harsh deserts, and the thick pads under their hooves enable them to tread on loose sand smoothly and steadily. The two-humped camels are much larger animals and walk more slowly than horses, but in arid regions they can endure much harsher conditions than horses can, and they can go without water and good pasture for much longer.

The extension of the Great Wall to this area also meant that this far-off border of the empire needed to be defended, but supplying these areas was expensive. In order to defend the new frontier efficiently and economically, the Han government established a new method of combining military garrisons with agricultural settlements. Soldiers went to the frontier along with their families, with agricultural equipment supplied by the government. The men and their families cultivated the land and maintained irrigation on the oases whenever there was no direct threat from north of the Great Wall. From around 100 BCE, when the

Han government started to implement the policy, the population of the oases increased steadily.

During the Han Dynasty, the first landmark for Chinese traders traveling westward was the Great Wall. At various places along it, watchtowers were built into it where Han soldiers who defended the frontier spent long nights and stored their belongings. Before the invention of paper, officers and soldiers kept documents about public business and wrote letters to their families on wooden slips. The thousands of wooden slips and tablets covered with Chinese characters that were left in the towers provide firsthand records of frontier life. However, it is not easy to get information from these wooden slips and tablets. A document or letter was created on a "page" made up of narrow wooden slips tied together with string. Then one or more pages could be rolled up and tied in a bundle. All one had to do to read the pages was to untie the outside string and unroll the slips. However, two millennia later, when archaeologists found these documents and letters, the strings that had bound the slips had completely disintegrated, and the slips and the tablets had become intermingled, forming many complex puzzles. Researchers have had to rearrange the slips and tablets in sequence to restore the documents.

The wooden tablets and books kept in the watchtowers had practical purposes. They have turned out to be records of commercial and legal transactions, including payrolls of soldiers, simple contracts, passports for travelers, official reports, and military orders, as well as family letters. Though many of the documents are fragmentary, they provide a glimpse of the frontier life of that era. For instance, the military payrolls tell us that soldiers were paid in bundles of plain silk textiles, which circulated as currency during Han times. Soldiers may well have traded their silk with the nomads who came to the gates of the Great Wall to sell horses and furs. Passports were issued to officials who traveled on public business and to private travelers, traders, and farmers who pursued their business inside and outside the Wall. These passports tell us that both official and private traders went to the frontier to buy horses.

Other information from the wooden slips has revealed that the soldiers assigned to a watchtower formed a combined military and farming unit. The head of the watchtower assigned a wide variety of jobs, including cooking, digging and repairing well-canals (an irrigation system including wells connected by underground canals), raising vegetables, cultivating crops, repairing tools, and herding stock to the soldiers, in addition to their duties as guards of the frontier. Officers and soldiers had to go through training to fulfill all these duties; they were also subject to regular inspections. A letter a petty officer wrote and left in a watchtower at Juyan, a gate of the Great Wall, reveals the affection he had for his beloved wife and his sense of duty as a frontier officer: "Yousun, my dear wife, your life is really hard....I hope you have enough food and clothing. If this is true, I feel happy at the frontier. Only because of the support of Yousun, Xuan can serve at the frontier faithfully, and have no need to worry about home."[9] The style of the writing and the calligraphy is poor, and there are many errors in the letter, but the feeling transcends these shortcomings.

Even in the oases west of the Gate of Jade—that is, west of the western end of the Han Dynasty's Great Wall—wooden tablets, inscribed in the Chinese language and in Chinese characters, sometimes were used as a media for diplomacy. In a wooden tablet that was part of a letter written in Chinese, found at a site on the southern edge of the Takla Makan Desert, the king of Dawan is helping the Yuezhi communicate with the Han emperor.[10] The Yuezhi either did not have a written language or had already adopted a local written language that was unintelligible to the Chinese. In order to address the Han ruler, they had to rely on the good services of the king of Dawan, who somehow had acquired a staff member in his court who could write in Chinese.

Chinese had become a language of crosscultural communication even outside the Great Wall because Chinese military frontier settlements, such as the ones in the Hexi Corridor, had been extended into areas outside the Gate of Jade. From the very name of the gate, one can guess that westward routes led from it to an actual source of jade: the Khotan region on the southern edge of the Takla Makan Desert. Although the jade trade through the Takla Makan Desert began in antiquity, long before the Qin and Han dynasties, the oasis settlements were still very small during the first century BCE. Without an efficient irrigation system, an oasis often could support only a few hundred households. The introduction of new Chinese agricultural technology and irrigation systems helped to increase the population of the oases all around the Takla Makan Basin. The number of households in small oases doubled or tripled, and those in large oases, such as Khotan, increased to many times their original number in about a century.[11] Improvements in agriculture and these population increases enabled the oases to support more commercial traffic through the Western

Regions (as the Chinese referred to Central Asia in general by this time). The larger the settlements were, the more food and fodder they could produce to supply the caravan traders and camels. In return, the caravan trade passing through these areas meant profits for their hosts. The oases became caravan cities, depending on the Silk Road trade for their prosperity.

During the chaotic period of dynastic transition from the Former Han to the Later Han, around the beginning of the Common Era, trade with the Western Regions suffered, whereas agriculture continued to thrive. Oasis states continued to grow and learned to contend with the harassments of the Xiongnu and other nomads. At the same time, the new oasis states fought for dominance. Tensions among the oases could also make the trade routes unsafe. The demand for western goods in the Han cities and an authority capable of maintaining order were necessary for the survival of the Central Asian trade. Eventually, the Han court resumed its control over the trade routes with the West in the mid-first century CE and sent several military missions to recover control of the parts of the Western Regions closest to China.

The Later Han Empire was a much weaker state than the Former Han and could only afford to send a limited military force into this remote area. Even that proved too costly for Emperor Zhangdi, who was ready to give up the region in 76 CE and ordered all military commanders to return to China from the Central Asian frontier. One of these generals, Ban Chao, remained there, however, with only a few hundred soldiers under his command, at the request of chiefs and people in oases such as Kashgar and Khotan, after obtaining the permission of the emperor. A capable military commander thoroughly familiar with local customs and languages, Ban Chao managed to maintain peace in the Western Regions; he protected the trade routes for more than three decades. His military achievements relied heavily on the cooperation of traders on the Silk Road. After his retirement from the Western Regions, his son, Ban Yong, who had grown up there, succeeded to the position of governor and continued to maintain Han control until the 120s CE. Although Han protection and authority weakened in the Western Regions after Ban Yong's tenure, the oasis states matured into stable, independent caravan cities. With reliable agricultural resources, they looked to caravans for their prosperity and developed into beautiful urban centers. Most of them remained hubs of commercial and cultural activities for many centuries.

Due to the arid climate of the Central Asian oases, many of the silk textiles made in China, in addition to some locally made ones, have survived in local burials there. Some of these samples are dated to the Han times; they range from lightweight tabby and gauze, some plain and some printed, to medium-textured fabrics—such as damask, in which the patterns are formed not by adding different colors but by weaving raised patterns over the material with the same color—and to the heaviest textiles, which included brocades, sometimes with raised designs of varied colors and sometimes with embroidery. The Han law code prohibited commoners, including traders, from wearing brocade and embroidered silks because the fabrics symbolized the wearer's status within the government and their production involved the greatest technology and skill. The looms during Han times were small, less than half a meter wide. To make polychrome brocade, the weaver arranged threads of various colors on the loom for the warp and then used the shuttle to weave in a weft of a single color. The patterns were sophisticated, but the pieces were small. The most common patterns on Han brocade were flowing clouds and motifs of animals such as geese, deer, and tigers. Chinese characters with auspicious meanings, such as longevity and prosperity, were often part of these designs. The rich religious and cultural textile remains of these caravan cities inspired many nineteenth-century European archaeologists and adventurers to explore these ancient trade routes, which they were the first to call "the Silk Road."

While Wudi was busy extending the Han Empire to the Western Regions, the Yuezhi moved their headquarters across the Oxus River and into what is now Afghanistan. The Kushan, one of the five tribes that formed the Yuezhi confederacy, unified all five to establish the Kushan kingdom. Chinese historical records refer to the Great Yuezhi as a country on a highland north of India where "the king calls himself 'Son of the Heaven.' The cavalry of the state is more than a hundred thousand in strength. The layout of the city and architecture are similar to that of the Romans."[12] In addition to Chinese texts, archaeological remains, including a treasury discovered in Begram, an ancient Kushan site, Kapisi, in Afghanistan, reveal an outline of this society. The Kushan kingdom established in this Hellenized region was a powerful and prosperous state. Its Greek architecture, complete with Corinthian columns, survived for many centuries; several hundred thousand beautiful horses roamed its pastures; and its people were skilled horse archers.

When the Yuezhi became rulers of agricultural societies on the Indian subcontinent during the first century CE, they also helped to further the fame of Chinese silk. In the Kushan kingdom, the former

In Han times, artisans who wove multicolored brocade fabrics liked to place auspicious characters for longevity and prosperity among lively animal motifs and floating cloud patterns. The typical Han brocade must have been in demand abroad, as many pieces have been excavated along the Silk Road in modern Xinjiang, such as this piece which was found in Loulan. Photograph by the author nomads, especially the rulers, were very well dressed, most likely in Chinese silk textiles. The many burial goods from six excavated tombs of Kushan princes in modern Afghanistan include more than 20,000 gold vessels, plates, and buckles, small remnants of decorative clothing, and other treasures, such as a bronze mirror from China and ivory carvings from India. The clothing began to disintegrate long ago, but it is possible to discern the style from the surviving gold buckles and decorative pieces sewn along the hems and seams, whose positions reveal the cut of the garments.[13] The Kushan princes and princesses wore knee-length robes and trousers in the steppe style, an indication that they continued to be an equestrian people, even after the Kushan became rulers of a sedentary society. The horse remained important in their rituals and ceremonies. While the cavalry remained the major military force for territorial expansion, horseback riding for the kings and princes living in the palaces was a symbol of royalty, just as it was in contemporary Han China.

Of all the foreign commodities brought to the gates of the Great Wall, the handsome horses from the western part of the Central Asian steppe were the goods most desired by the Han court. After several hundred years of interactions with nomads, sedentary rulers not only had come to understand the advantage of cavalry in warfare but also had started to appreciate equestrian culture as an imperial style. By the first century CE, horses had acquired great significance in parades of power. The horse-drawn chariot, an outmoded form in warfare, had become the moving throne of rulers, human and divine. Only gods and kings were shown riding in chariots when hunting or fighting. In the royal tombs of the Han time, figurines of cavalry outnumber those of infantry. The Han emperor Wudi craved the spectacularly beautiful horses in the westernmost part of the Western Regions. A breed known as "blood-sweating horses," which according to legend had been interbred with heavenly horses, came from Dawan. In addition to their breeding, the horses also benefited from the mild climate and high grasses of the Central Asian steppe, which was friendlier to livestock than the Mongolian steppe. Central Asians had also learned to feed horses with alfalfa, a very nutritious species of grass.

Wudi first tried to obtain these superior horses by sending out an envoy who offered to buy them with large quantities of gold and silk. However, the king of Dawan was not just unwilling to trade horses, which he considered the special treasure of the state—he killed the Han envoy! In response to this insult, a military expedition headed by

General Li Guangli set off to conquer Dawan in 104 BCE. His army experienced great difficulties crossing the deserts and steppes and had many casualties during its first attempt. The emperor, nevertheless, was determined to own the so-called heavenly horses. When Li's expeditionary forces retreated to the Great Wall, Wudi had Li stopped at the Gate of Jade and ordered the guards to kill any soldier who tried to come through. Li turned his army around, went back to Uzbekistan, eventually killed the king of Dawan, and brought back 3,000 heavenly horses.[14] Such heavenly horses thereafter became the royal symbol of the Han Empire. Even today, in the vicinity of the city of Xi'an—the modern site of the Han capital, Chang'an—next to the monumental tomb of the emperor Wudi a large, muscular stone horse triumphantly tramples a defeated Xiongnu.

The heavenly horses came from a country rich in not only horses and alfalfa but also grapes and wine. Remains of Hellenistic garrison towns in Uzbekistan suggest that the people of Dawan had learned to raise grapes and make wine. Wealthy households stored more than 10,000 jars of grape wine apiece. In the first century CE, Ban Gu, the compiler of the *Official History of the Former Han Dynasty*, wrote: "The Son of Heaven [the Han emperor] knew there were many heavenly horses and many foreign visitors and thus had alfalfa and grapes planted in various palaces and villas on large plots of land."[15] In Han China, grapes and alfalfa graced palaces and public places and became very popular plants, but there is no evidence of grape wine consumption during this period.

For the Han elite, the exquisite products from the West inspired a curiosity about and admiration for the Roman Empire. On the site of Loulan at the northeast edge of the Takla Makan Desert, in the same place where many Han silk textiles were excavated, archaeologists found a fragment of a woolen tapestry showing half of a man's face that is strikingly Roman in artistic style and physical features. This kind of artwork was probably the sort of woolen textile the Han elites desired, including both the royal family and the literati-officials. General Ban Chao sent an envoy to the Romans to learn about this rich and large empire at the other end of the trade routes. This envoy, Gan Ying, traveled all the way to the coast of the "West Sea"—possibly the Persian Gulf—but failed to reach Rome. When he reached the port city he called "Tiaozhi," which was under the control of the Parthians, a powerful dynasty based in Iran, local people told him that the sea voyage from there to Rome was far too dangerous and would require several more years to accomplish, and he was persuaded to give up the trip. In the lands between the Mediterranean and the Persian Gulf, agents of both the Romans and Parthians profited from the trade that moved along the Silk Road. These merchants included those who plied the Red Sea and the Arabian Sea, and those who traveled overland from oasis to oasis. They had the most to lose from any direct Chinese contact with Rome, and presumably they were eager to discourage such ties.

CHAPTER 2

Rome Looks East

In the first century CE, the Roman scholar Pliny the Elder shared what he thought he knew about China and silk in his encyclopedia *Natural History*: "the Chinese...are famous for the woolen substance obtained from their forests; after a soaking in water they comb off the white down of the leaves, and so supply our women with the double task of unraveling the threads and weaving them together again."[1] That he in fact knew relatively little about silk is not surprising, since it was only during his lifetime that the Silk Road trade first began to deliver large quantities of silk to Roman markets. Indeed, he claimed that so much Chinese silk and other luxuries from distant parts of Asia were being purchased in Roman markets that the treasury of the empire was bleeding: wealthy Roman women were buying so many fine silk fabrics to adorn themselves that Rome's supply of bullion was being depleted. His statement that "trees bear wool" seems to refer to cotton plants (which are actually bushes, not trees), or silk-cotton trees, which really are trees that produce kapok, silky fibers similar to silk floss. Neither of these plants produces silk, and both are actually native to India, not China. Learned Romans such as Pliny the Elder did not know much about these products because traders did not need to travel very far east to purchase silks and other luxuries. Roman traders made their purchases at depots near the eastern side of the Mediterranean. Traders of various Asian nationalities traveled the silk routes to caravan cities near the Mediterranean to supply these Roman depots with such things as silks from China and spices from India.

When the Roman Republic evolved into the Roman Empire during the first century BCE, life in Rome and other major cities changed. The ever expanding empire incorporated all sorts of people and goods from the Mediterranean coasts and further east. In the first century CE, at the same time that the oases around the Takla Makan Desert were developing into caravan cities, the Roman emperors and wealthy citizens took great interest in the products brought to them from caravan cities on the edges of the Syrian and Jordanian deserts. Unlike the Chinese Han government, which promoted the development of oases to defend the western trade routes, the Romans inherited their eastern trade routes

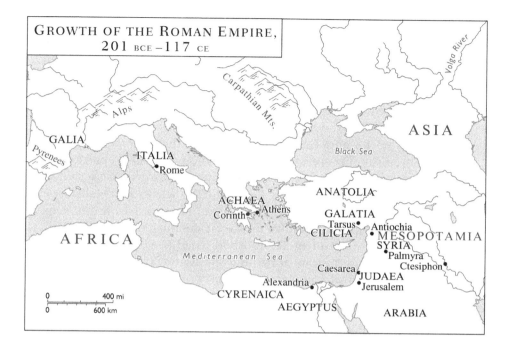

GROWTH OF THE ROMAN EMPIRE,
201 BCE – 117 CE

from the earlier Hellenistic powers and the Arabs. The caravan cities in Arabic-speaking lands had been established long before the arrival of the Romans or the silks. However, the rise of Rome as an imperial power created a large market for the goods carried by the overland camel trade. Spices, perfumes, and silk—the newest, most luxurious textile (which during the Roman era was made mostly in China)—became the most valuable items. The expansion of the Roman Empire meant new goods for its wealthy citizens and greater prosperity for the empire as a whole. The Roman Empire had therefore a keen interest in protecting eastern caravan routes, with the result that it placed a new emphasis on its frontier in the Middle East.

During the last two centuries before the Common Era, when the Han Empire was busy dealing with the Xiongnu and other nomads on its northern borders, the Romans themselves were mostly contending with Carthage in northern Africa and the Celts and Germans in Europe. Rome began to pay more attention to the eastern Mediterranean region after the mid-first century BCE, as Ptolemaic Egypt, a Hellenistic state ruled by a Greek dynasty, became its primary area of strategic interest.

In the same period, the political structure of the Levant, the eastern Mediterranean coastal civilizations, also changed dramatically, in part due to migrations of nomadic groups from the Eurasian steppe. The conflicts on the Mongolian steppe had a pinball effect, starting a series of nomadic migrations from the borders of China all the way to the Middle East and almost as far as the Mediterranean. The military and political situation of the Roman Empire also had an impact on trade relations in the Levant. Ancient kingdoms on the Arabian Peninsula had long been suppliers of spices and fragrances (incense in particular) to the Mediterranean market. The Arab traders, however, were caught in the crossfire between Ptolemaic Egypt and the Seleucids, a Hellenistic state in Mesopotamia. Both dynasties were descended from the generals who had helped Alexander the Great conquer the Middle East, Afghanistan, and parts of India, and both tried to control Phoenicia, access to the Mediterranean ports, and the Red Sea routes to Arabia and India.[2] Their rival commercial interests often brought them into military conflict.

The greatest threat to the Seleucids, however, was not Egypt but the Parthians, the nomadic people originally based just north of Iran, who had begun expanding their own empire into Seleucid-held territory during the third century BCE. During the next century, the Parthian Empire expanded westward under pressure of the Sakas, another nomadic group that had arisen on the steppe and begun migrating westward. The Sakas, in their turn, had moved to the west under pressure from the Yuezhi, who had been forced to flee from a region near the Chinese border by the Xiongnu around the 130s BCE.

The Parthians defeated the Seleucid regime around 64 BCE. Egypt became a Roman province after the death of Cleopatra, the Ptolemaic queen, in 30 BCE. Rome's new eastern frontier in the Middle East now faced the Parthian Empire based in Iran. The inevitable clash of the Romans and the Parthians along their shared frontier arose not only out of strategic issues but also out of competition over commercial goods and profits.

In spite of the contending empires, trade in the Levant was still firmly in the hands of Arabs and other peoples who spoke related Semitic languages. They had lived and traded there for many centuries, despite the changing political fortunes of the Greeks, Parthians, and Romans. Despite their lack of arable land, the leaders of the ancient Arabs were not poor, primarily because they were good traders controlling profitable land and sea routes. The Persian Gulf gave access to Mesopotamia, the Red Sea to the coast of northeastern Africa, and the Isthmus of Suez to Egypt and the Mediterranean. Moreover, towns on the Arabian Sea were linked by sea routes to the bountiful ports of India. Arab traders navigated the deserts with the camel, "the ship of the desert," and the sea with the dhow, a fast and sturdy sailing craft. Arabs relied on their camels for transportation so much that they never invented or adopted the wheel as other ancient peoples did.[3] Arabs had sailed their dhows on the Indian Ocean from time immemorial. Their triangular sails could be pivoted and could handle winds from various directions much better than the rectangular sails common in other waters of the world. Their hulls were made of planks of teak, a hardwood imported from India, and the planks were tied together with a fibrous rope.[4] However, the dhow, though available in various sizes, was often smaller than other seafaring ships.

Deserts limited agricultural production on the Arabian Peninsula. The one exception to this was the southeast coast (more or less in present-day Yemen), which produced the two fragrances most in demand in the ancient world, frankincense and myrrh, which are made from tree resins. Before the Silk Road brought great quantities of luxuries from East Asia, Arabian frankincense and myrrh were the most desired and expensive goods in Mediterranean markets. The Greeks and Romans used large amounts of frankincense and myrrh not only in the worship of their gods and goddesses but also in the burials of the dead. In the early first millennium BCE, the Sabaean state, renowned throughout the Middle East for its frankincense and myrrh, ruled the region. According to the Hebrew Bible, King Solomon of Israel received a visiting queen named Sheba, who brought him fabulous gifts: "When the queen of Sheba heard of the name of Solomon, she came to test him with hard questions. She came to Jerusalem with a very great retinue, with camels bearing spices and very much gold, and precious stones" (1 Kings 10:1–2). This queen was probably from the Sabaean kingdom.

In the New Testament, three magi, often referred to as wise men from the East, went to Bethlehem to pay their respects to the newborn Jesus: "On entering the house, they saw the child with Mary his mother; and they knelt down and paid him homage. Then opening their treasure chests, they offered him gifts of gold, frankincense, and myrrh" (Matt. 2:11). By this time, the Himyarites, another tribe of the peninsula, had built a kingdom and inherited the Sabaean culture of southern Arabia. During the first century CE, when Roman traders were sailing to India via the Red Sea and the Arabian Sea, they stopped in Himyarite ports on the way in order to purchase the fragrant resins that they could sell at a profit in India.

Frankincense and myrrh traveled routes that went northwest toward Egypt and the coastal cities of the Mediterranean. At that time, a people known as the Nabataeans, who lived in northwestern Arabia, controlled the part of the caravan trade that passed through their territory. In the fourth century BCE, before they became involved in the caravan trade, the Nabataeans were sheep-herders who prospered among barren red sandstone hills, mountains, and ravines. To preserve rainwater, they skillfully excavated large cisterns in solid rock, a key to survival in the harsh climate of the Arabian deserts.

Between the 100s BCE and the first century CE, as the Parthians and the Romans clashed over the remnant of Seleucid power in Syria, traders took safer routes that avoided the battlefields along the Euphrates River. After Roman generals finally annexed Syria, around 63 BCE, Mesopotamia became a war zone for these two empires, and portions of the Euphrates River changed possession back and forth between them. The Nabataeans settled down to take advantage of the passing trade in a Jordanian ravine, between the Dead Sea and the Gulf of Aqaba, a bay of the Red Sea. They either pitched tents or sought shelter in rock caves. They began by supplying water and food to caravans passing through the valley, and then they built strongholds on the mountaintops to defend their settlements. In the third century BCE, they maintained their independence against the expansion of both the Ptolemies of Egypt and the Seleucids of Mesopotamia. With the wealth accumulated from their trade, they displayed their prosperity by building the splendid caravan city of Petra (Greek for "rock"), named for the rose-colored stone they used to build it. Both the living and the dead were housed in rock caves adorned on the outside with columns fashioned in the Greek style. Located in a strategically important valley that provided a passage through the mountains, Petra controlled this critical incense trade route from southern Arabia to cities on the Mediterranean coast.

The route leading to the city of Petra is called Wadi Moussa in Arabic, which means the Valley of Moses. Approaching the city from the peninsula's southern coast, trade caravans first encountered the monumental façades of the burial caves. On the left side of the valley, the caravan trader would see a huge tomb complex, marked by four monolithic obelisks glowing red under the Arabian sun. The road soon turned into a narrow gorge, probably cut by floods, where the Nabataeans had ingeniously protected themselves from the danger of flooding by building a dam and dikes to divert the waters. The caravans continued through a gorge that Arabs called the Siq. Flanked by high cliffs, the gorge was so narrow that only a thread of light could penetrate to the

Khasneh is the first shrine to welcome visitors to Petra, a caravan city in the rock valley of the Dead Sea, in Jordan. Today the sculpture of the central deity is too defaced to show its exact identity, but the conical roof above the shrine, supported by Greek style columns, shows that Petreans added their own architectural imprints on the Hellenistic façade of the city. Library of Congress, LC-DIG0matpc-04475 ground. A group of statues representing a caravan—robed men leading camels—from the first century BCE or CE, when Petra flourished, stands at the spring of the Siq. Because of erosion, only the hooves of the camels and the lower parts of the human figures have survived. These statues, twice life-size, were road markers that guided the caravan traders proceeding through the dark valley in the direction of the shining city of Petra.

Once through the dark passage, the sudden splendor of the façade of the huge temple of Khasneh would have dazzled the eyes of the traders. At the first level of the façade, six Corinthian columns supported the roof. Above the roof were three niches, also flanked by Corinthian columns, that rose almost as tall as those on the first level. Over the centuries, erosion has damaged the statues of the three deities housed in the niches. The main deity in the middle is obviously a female; the other two are probably male gods. Whatever the nature and the name of the goddess, she must have been one of the major protectors of caravans and the caravan city.

After the Khasneh, the valley widened. To the left of the road, the Nabataeans' sacred place of sacrifice, at the top of the highest mountain in the region, rose high above its summit. Nabataean priests most likely communicated with their supreme god there, from an altar open to the sky. On a nearby hilltop, two obelisks represented the gods of the sun and the moon. Following the road westward, very close to the road, the caravan trader would have seen an amphitheater carved out of rose-colored sandstone. It had forty-five rows of seats, divided into three horizontal sectors. The orchestra pit was a perfect semicircle, following the cultural influence of Rome. After the traveler passed this theater, the valley opened up into a basin. On the right one could then see, far away, a façade of Corinthian columns, adorned with uniquely Petraean conical tops, along the red sandstone cliffs. On the left, where the stream that was diverted above now joined the Wadi Moussa—the Valley of Moses—one finally reached the urban area of Petra.

A typical entrance in cities built in the Hellenistic style of the time greeted the traveler on first walking into the city: a shrine to the left and a *nymphaeum*, a structure with a fountain and a statue, to the right. Along the main street was arrayed a colonnade of freestanding red sandstone columns that extended for about three hundred yards along the river flowing through the Wadi Moussa. Shops and hotels with colonnaded porticos lined the main street; behind them, rows of houses climbed into the foothills. On the main street, monumental buildings dominated the scene. Three elevated platforms served as markets for the traders. On the other side of the main street, opposite the market, stood the royal palace. Two major temples flanked the west end of the colonnade, which was marked by a huge gate decorated with bas-relief. From there, the traveler could see the largest shrine of the city to the west.

The ancient Nabataeans worshiped various gods from different cultures. Greek, Roman, Mesopotamian, Persian, and Egyptian art all influenced the statues of gods and goddesses in Nabataean shrines. One statue in the Greek style might represent Zeus, whereas another one might be dedicated to the worship of a local deity. The ancient Nabataeans left no written record of their religious life, but the material remains of their religious practices reveal a cosmopolitan view of the world and of an afterlife. Still, under the veneer of Greco-Roman art, and despite trace influences of Persia, Egypt, and Mesopotamia, traditional Nabataean traders were firmly attached to their own gods. The two major deities, Dusares and al-Uzza, the Sun and the Moon, were most likely the lords in the largest temple.[5]

The nature of caravan trade helped shape the cosmopolitan views of the residents of Petra. Most of them, especially the men, spoke both the local language and Greek. The scripts and inscriptions of the city were mostly in the local (Semitic) Petraean language, a tongue closely related to Arabic, although the Nabataeans used Greek military and administrative titles and the Greek alphabet when dealing with their Hellenistic subjects in the north.

The economy of Petra, as a caravan city surrounded by powerful rival regimes, fluctuated with political events. From 164 BCE to the time of Trajan in the early second century CE, the Greeks and Romans knew the names of prominent citizens of Petra. The merchant-rulers of Petra controlled the main Spice Road, the name given by modern historians to the trade routes supplying spices, incense, and textiles from Arabia, Africa, and India. Petraean merchants reached as far west as Phoenicia on the southeast coast of the Mediterranean and even settled in their own trading communities, with their own temples, in Italy.[6]

In the second century CE, Petra's fortunes began to decline. Among scholars, there is little agreement as to why. Petra's reliance on the spice trade and passing caravans must have made it vulnerable to changes in commercial routes. Petra prepared for the coming of the Roman Empire's eastern trade. Its decline came about after the growth of the Silk Road trade, both by sea from India and over land through Parthia, and with the rise of the greatest of all the Middle Eastern trading centers, Palmyra.

Palmyra was a marble city built at the site of an oasis in the Syrian desert, approximately halfway between the Mediterranean and the Euphrates River. The colonnade of Palmyra was more magnificent, and its temples grander than those of Petra or any other Middle Eastern caravan city. Palmyra, essentially the easternmost entrance to the Roman market, has attracted a large number of archaeological explorations and research projects, which have revealed abundant information about the Silk Road trade.[7] A bilingual inscription called the Tariff of Palmyra tells us exactly how much duty was charged on specific goods carried by the caravans. Archaeological excavations have revealed that many silk textiles from Han China reached this site and that many were buried in the graves of Palmyra. These excavated silk samples provide the first material evidence of the arrival of the silk trade in the Mediterranean region.

The rise of Palmyra to a position of dominance was, to a great extent, the result of competition and compromise between the Roman and the Parthian empires, the two powerhouses in the central part of Eurasia. Before Roman influence reached the oasis settlement that became Palmyra, it was called Tadmor. The name "Palmyra," meaning "city of palm trees," was given to it by the Romans. Roman Palmyra nevertheless maintained its autonomy as a frontier city. Because the caravan trade was in the common interest of both empires, Palmyra profited by trading with both the Parthians and the Romans. As middlemen, the merchants of Palmyra benefited first from the spice route linking the Arabian Peninsula to the Mediterranean, and then from the silk route linking China to the West.

Prior to the arrival of the Romans and Parthians in this area, the Palmyraean region had been under a Hellenistic Seleucid regime, which meant that Greek influence was even more apparent in Palmyra than in Petra, which always remained independent of outside powers.[8] Palmyra's Grand Colonnade, which was on the main thoroughfare, was at the center of its urban area. More than 375 Corinthian columns lined each side of this avenue. At its eastern end, the colonnade was marked by a great gate with three arches. On the south side of the grand avenue stood three huge public water fountains, the agora, the Senate house, and the theater. This area provided all the basic infrastructure of a Greek city.

The admiration for Greek-style architecture and institutions, however, did not mean that Palmyra's people had abandoned their local culture. In the sanctuary area of the city, its great temple was dedicated to the Semitic deity Bel. Palmyraeans worshiped Bel along with Yarhibol and Aglibol, the gods of the Sun and the Moon. Together these three gods formed the main spiritual triad of the city. Palmyraeans worshiped other gods as well, including the Semitic god Baal Shamin. Local shrines also had a place in the ritual life of the city. Many of the deities worshiped there had assumed Greek names but were probably of Middle Eastern origin. This blending of gods eastern and western, old and new, was possible because classical Greek religious beliefs were not exclusive, and room could always be made for new deities. This inclusiveness in Greek religion had helped to create unity among very different conquered populations in the wake of the military conquests of Alexander the Great in the fourth century BCE. In addition, despite Greek titles, most gods in Palmyra retained their original Semitic features. In their daily lives, the Palmyraeans spoke their native language, a Semitic dialect related to Arabic and Hebrew. For the most part, Greek was used when dealing with official business and for some special occasions.

Outside the urban area of Palmyra was a large necropolis. The sculptures dedicated to those buried there were as elaborate and artistic as those designed for the living in other parts of the city. The wealthy Palmyraeans invested a great deal of their wealth in the buildings that housed their dead because they believed in a life after death that was similar to the deceased's life before death. The statues were so beautifully done that many have been taken from the sites and displayed in museums all over the world. The necropolis serves as a mirror of life in Palmyra. On numerous grand tombs, the masters, lying on Greek-style couches, often hold goblets in their hands. Relatives of the buried may have held celebrations in front of these tombs and enjoyed drinking with the spirits of their deceased family members.

The couches, drinking vessels, and hairstyles might be Hellenistic, but the long robes that clothe these figures are similar to those of the Parthians. These robes carved in marble are often decorated with exquisite designs, probably representing the textiles Palmyraeans actually wore. Rich merchants in this trading center enjoyed what they considered to be the best of the material cultures from all directions. From the West, Hellenization brought wine drinking, viticulture, and olive oil. Scenes of drinking and motifs of grapes and grape leaves appear on many works of art. Luxurious clothing and textiles from the East also found a market here.

Around the grand tombs stand numerous sculptures depicting camel caravans, and occasionally a horse appears in one of these scenes. The camel and the horse met as pack animals at Palmyra. The caravan god Arsu probably came from Arabian deserts and was depicted as a soldier riding on a camel, whereas the god Azizu came from the land of those

A noble couple attends a funeral feast in this stone relief from the tombs in the necropolis of Palmyra, Syria. Many sculptures there reflect actual events during Palmyra's golden days as the eastern trading depot of the Roman Empire. Erich Lessing / Art Resource, NY

who rode on horseback. According to their tombstones, even in death the merchant princes engaged in caravan trade.

Palmyraean merchant caravans carried many textiles, including silks. Archaeological excavations in Palmyra have turned up more than five hundred pieces of textiles, including linen, wool, cotton, and silk.[9] While most linen was probably produced locally, cotton was imported, most likely from India. Among the woolen textiles, cashmere was definitely a product of Kashmir or some other highland region in Central Asia. Silk textiles were mostly produced in Han China, but the remains of silk yarns and dyes indicate that people in the Middle East had started to weave silk textiles out of imported silk yarns. By this time, some of these silk textiles woven outside of China appear to have been fabricated anywhere between the Mediterranean and Central Asia. One piece of silk, woven using Chinese technology, depicts Central Asian scenes, including one of men harvesting grapes with two humped camels in the background.[10] The existence of this piece of silk in Palmyra raises the question of how far west the Chinese technology of silk weaving had traveled by this time. The piece of silk may reflect scenes from oasis cities in Chinese Central Asia, where silk weaving had already spread during the Han Dynasty, camels had been used for many thousands of years, and viticulture had already spread from the West.

The commercial network of Palmyra extended far beyond the oasis and all the way to the Persian Gulf. The city also provided financial services to caravans and sent merchants to faraway lands where they set up trading sites called *fonduq*. These communities included a caravanserai: a compound with a hostel for the traders and their animals, storage buildings for their merchandise, offices, and often a temple. Most Palmyraean trading outposts were in cities under Parthian rule, such as Babylon and Vologesia, and others further south near the mouth of the Euphrates and Tigris rivers.

Palmyraean traders sent ships and representatives to the ports of both the Parthians, their suppliers, and the Romans, who ruled over their major markets. The head of the fonduq in Vologesia had a temple constructed in honor of the Roman emperor Hadrian.[11] It seems rather ironic that the merchants of Palmyra worshiped Roman emperors within the bounds of Parthia, Rome's foremost enemy at that time. Their attachment to Roman deities also suggests that their commercial and spiritual loyalties were tied to the West rather than the East. Hadrian was worshiped because as emperor of Rome he had restored both peace and trade in this frontier region. Roman suzerainty over this caravan empire and, more important, the Roman market for the goods Palmyra obtained from the East were vital to the city's survival.

Important merchants, including the heads of merchant clans, managers of trading outposts, and heads of caravans composed the ruling elite of Palmyra. Four clans were the most prestigious among dozens of Palmyraean trading families, but it is unclear how they attained the leadership of this commercial empire. They apparently still organized their political life after the manner of the Greeks, as is demonstrated by the architecture of the urban area in Palmyra. The agora, the senate building, and the theater were all for public gatherings. (The theater was not just a place for the performance of Greek dramas but also was used for meetings of the local citizenry.) Most likely, the most powerful—including heads of clans, top merchants and caravan leaders—and the more general members of the public all gathered together in Palmyra's outwardly Greek buildings.

Under the leadership of the mercantile oligarchy, Palmyra flourished from the second to the third century. The Roman Empire generally did not interfere in the city's affairs until another major threat came from the east. The Sassanid Dynasty, a new regime based in southern Iran that replaced Parthian rule in southern Mesopotamia in 227 CE, disrupted the old balance of power in the region. Even more eager to confront Rome than the Parthians had been, the Sassanids blocked the Roman trading route to the Persian Gulf and disrupted the commerce of both Palmyra and Rome. Septimius Odaenathus, a local Palmyraean who became the ruler of the city's trading empire as the representative of Rome on its eastern frontier, successfully pushed back the invasion of the Sassanids in the year 267. When he and his son, the heir apparent, died in the same year, his second wife Zenobia became the queen of the kingdom.

It was said that Zenobia was among the few non-Romans there who spoke some Latin and who had her sons educated in Latin. Besides being capable, she was ambitious. Rumor had it that she murdered her husband and the son of his first wife in order to secure the throne for Wahballat, her own son. Wahballat assumed both the Persian-style title "king of kings" and the Roman post of "governor of all the East." Zenobia quickly expanded the territory of her kingdom at the expense of the Roman Empire. In 269, the Palmyraean army occupied Egypt and within the same year a large part of Anatolia. She then declared Palmyra independent from Rome. The Roman emperor, Aurelian, had no choice but to send Roman troops to suppress the rebellion. He defeated the Palmyraean army at Immae, near Antioch, and then besieged Palmyra itself in 272.[12] Zenobia was captured after the Roman siege of her city, and she and her son were taken prisoner by the victors.

The Romans would probably have left Palmyra alone had Zenobia been satisfied with the title and power of the queen mother and not attacked Egypt and Anatolia. In Rome, according to legend, she was forced to march in gold chains before the emperor's chariot in the triumphal procession held in 274. The event aroused the curiosity and fascination of Roman citizens, and this woman from the mysterious city of Palmyra was imprinted in their memories. The image of Zenobia, like that of Cleopatra several centuries earlier, lived on in the memory of the Romans as a symbol of the power and ambition of female rulers in the East. The glory of Palmyra as a wealthy trading city ended one year later, after a second unsuccessful rebellion against Rome.

The prosperity of Palmyra in the second and third centuries had depended very much on the entrepôt of Dura, a city on the Euphrates River, on the frontier between Rome and Parthia. Commercial and strategic conditions in Dura affected business in Palmyra and the whole of Roman Syria. Rome understood Dura's importance and exercised tighter control over it than over Palmyra.

As a town, Dura existed from around 280 BCE to 256 CE. It began as a Macedonian garrison; Greek soldiers under Alexander settled there and built a polis. The soldiers soon married the local Semitic women, who made their own culture a part of local urban life. After the Parthians became masters of Mesopotamia and Dura in the mid-second century BCE, it became a garrison town of the Parthians that stood against the Romans. Thereafter, images of Parthian cavalry on galloping horses appeared on the walls of Dura.[13] Soon an Iranian population blended in, bringing their clothing styles and other material culture. In 165 CE, the Romans took over Dura and renamed it Europus. For the Romans, Dura-Europus, their easternmost garrison, was a strategic outpost that guaranteed the safety of trade routes between the Euphrates and the Mediterranean. Roman soldiers ruled the town. Their commanders had an elaborate bath built to make the soldiers feel at home, although many of them came from places outside the Italian peninsula and had never been to Rome. In the middle of the third century, the Romans lost Dura to the Sassanids, and they were never able to recover it. Although the rise of the Sassanid Empire seriously affected Roman traders' profits from the eastern goods that arrived via the land routes, the Roman market for these luxuries had also begun to decline at that time. Dura, along with other caravan cities in Syria and Jordan, was eventually buried by desert sands and lay hidden until modern archaeologists found them in the early twentieth century.

While Palmyra, Dura, and Petra flourished, the Romans already had an alternate route for obtaining silk and other luxuries from the East: sea routes that connected Egypt's Red Sea coast with the Persian Gulf and the western coast of the Indian subcontinent. Indeed, there is some evidence that from the first to fourth centuries BCE, sailors from Ptolemaic Egypt, prior to the Roman takeover of Egypt, used such routes. Eventually, the Han Chinese became aware of these markets. The *History of the Later Han*, which covers the history of the dynasty during the first two centuries CE, mentions that both Parthia and India traded with the Romans "at sea," and that the trade was very lucrative.[14] The Parthians may have traded with the Romans—or, most likely, with their Palmyraean or Duran agents—at Persian Gulf ports, whence goods were brought up the Euphrates River. The Roman-Indian sea trade probably originated in the western ports of the subcontinent and extended from there to Red Sea ports in Roman-controlled Egypt.

At least as early as the first century BCE, Greek-Egyptians had become interested in goods from India. The Greek-Egyptians first learned about the potential of Indian Ocean trade from an Indian who had ventured up the Nile. The Indian, who almost perished during his adventures, told Eudoxus of Cyzicus, an adventurer in the second century BCE, about the route to India and the wealth in that country that could be found across the Arabian Sea.[15] After Eudoxus returned from a voyage to India, other Greek-Egyptian sailors also made trips to the subcontinent. The story comes from Strabo, the Greek geographer of the first century BCE, who also stated that "when Gallus was prefect of Egypt, I accompanied him and ascended the Nile...and I learned that as many as 120 vessels were sailing from Myos Hormos to India, whereas formerly, under the Ptolemies, only a very few ventured to undertake the voyage and to carry on traffic in Indian merchandise."[16]

Maritime trade on the Red Sea and the Arabian Sea expanded even faster after the Romans took control of these routes in their search for the silks that were available in the ports of western India. The Romans did not know of the silks' Chinese origins. At some point in the mid-first century CE, a Greek manual on navigation from the Red Sea to India appeared. The anonymous author of this work, the *Periplus of the Red Sea*, was a sailor or captain who often traveled between the Red Sea and India. He claimed that a sailor named Hippalus had discovered how to ride the monsoon winds, which enabled a ship to reach India and return back to the Red Sea within a year's time.[17] The monsoon winds on the Arabian Sea blow southeast from April to October, and northwest from October to April. Taking advantage of this wind, a ship could sail on the high seas directly to India and back, instead of clinging to the coast and going from port to port all along the southern edge of the Arabian Peninsula and the Makran coast, the coastal region of Arabian Sea in southern Iran.

The sailors on the Red Sea during Roman times were descendants of Greeks who had become established in Egypt during Ptolemaic times. Some partial knowledge of the monsoon had probably been available to these earlier sailors, and there is no doubt that the Arabs and Indians figured out this wind pattern even earlier. The word "monsoon" is derived from Arabic. However, as the incentive for Indian trade became stronger in Roman times, voyages east became more frequent, more specific knowledge of the monsoon trade winds became imperative to regularizing trade with India, and the *Periplus of the Red Sea* was published.

Even though the quickest way to reach India by sea was to ride the monsoon winds directly across the Arabian Sea to India's western coast, in practice traders visited various commercial ports on the coasts of the Arabian Peninsula and southern Iran. Frankincense and myrrh from southern Arabia had always been in demand in the Mediterranean, and these commodities would also fetch good prices in India. The profits Roman traders made from selling Arabian incense in India enabled them to purchase even more goods while they were on the subcontinent. The *Periplus* provides detailed information both about the sea routes to India, including the use of the winds, and about what traders could sell there and what they could expect to buy in all the ports around the Arabian Sea:

> The port of trade of Muza, though without a harbor, offers a good roadstead for mooring because of the anchorages with sandy bottom all around. Merchandise for which it offers a market are: purple cloth, fine and ordinary quality; Arab sleeved clothing, either with no adornment or with the common adornment or with checks or interwoven with gold thread; saffron; *cyperus* [no translation found]; cloth; *abollai* [no translation found]; blankets, in limited number, with no adornment as well as with traditional local adornment; girdles with shaded stripes; unguent, moderate amount; money, considerable amount; wine and grain, limited quantity because the region produces wheat in moderate quantity and wine in greater.... Its exports consist of local products—myrrh...white marble—as well as all the aforementioned merchandise from Adulis across the water. The best time for sailing to this place is around the month of September...though there is nothing to prevent leaving even earlier.[18]

The *Periplus* contains much useful information for both ship captains and traders, and it is probable that most ship captains were also traders in those days. From the Mediterranean, they sailed up the Nile and then portaged to the Red Sea. The author of the *Periplus* does not tell us what kinds of goods the Roman ships were carrying when they left the Red Sea ports, but judging from the goods he suggests would sell well in foreign lands, the cargo most likely included such Mediterranean products as grape wine, various vessels associated with wine drinking, jars of olive oil, glassware, coral, woolen and linen textiles and clothing, and artworks made of metal, including bronze, brass, silver and gold. Gold coins from the Mediterranean region were also essential, and have been found in many ports of India and other countries along the routes described in the *Periplus*.

During Ptolemaic times, traders would have stopped along the southern half of Africa's Red Sea coastline and at ports along the Horn of Africa. The Romans called this coast—from present-day Sudan to Somalia—"Berber country," another word for "barbarian," and mainly stopped there to buy elephants and ivory.[19] The *Periplus* refers to the peoples of these areas by names such as "fish eaters" and "calf eaters." Market towns along the African coast welcomed goods the Romans brought, such as robes and cloaks made in Egypt, copper drinking vessels, raw copper or brass for making utensils and ornaments, and glassware. Wines from Italy and Laodicea, a city in Roman Syria, were also sold there. To balance this trade, the Romans still had to pay some cash in the form of their silver and gold coins. This region also imported Indian products, such as cotton textiles, as well as iron and steel items for hunting elephants. Roman sailors frequently encountered Arab and Indian ships in these ports and nearby waters. This part of Africa not only exported elephants, ivory, tortoise shells, and slaves but also spices such as cinnamon and aromatic woods such as myrrh and frankincense. Frankincense from these African ports was referred to as the "far side" variety. The author the *Periplus* calls the Horn of Africa the Cape of Spices, and that was the extent of Roman knowledge of Africa's eastern seaboard.

The ports of Arabia were a more important market for the sailors than those on the African coast. At the Red Sea's northern end, inland from the coast, lay Nabataean country, with Petra as its capital.[20] By the time of the *Periplus*, Petra was under the protection of the Roman Empire, and the Roman troops who resided there claimed one-fourth of the imported merchandise as tribute. Unhappy with this arrangement, many Nabataeans resorted to piracy. The *Periplus* notes that some inland people, "speaking two languages, who are vicious," often seized passing ships.[21] We know the Nabataeans in Petra, who spoke both their local tongue and Greek, had had a monopoly on spices and fragrances for centuries before the Romans' arrival.

When the ships reached the western coast of modern Yemen, at the southern end of the Red Sea, the author of the *Periplus* tells us, they would encounter Muza, a south Arabian market town.[22] Arab ships crowded this port to trade with merchants from the "far side" coast and from Barygaza, an Indian port on the Gulf of Cambay. Although the southwestern part of Arabia was under the rule of the Himyarites at this time, the local Sabaean tribes still managed the production of frankincense and myrrh. This region was no doubt the largest source for these treasured fragrances, supplying both the land and sea routes.

The local traders of Muza were very affluent, and one could not get away with purchasing the goods there with cheap trinkets, as the Greek and Roman traders often did when dealing with the "berbers" on the African coast. The merchants of Muza imported all kinds of textiles, fine or coarse, including cloth colored purple with a special dye of the eastern Mediterranean. The wealthy among them dressed in the Arabian style, in textiles embroidered or woven with gold thread. The Arabs in Muza imported some wine, but not a great amount, as there was a plentiful supply of wine made from locally available dates. The kings and the chiefs often wanted something special to demonstrate their royalty—horses and pack mules, gold and silver plates, copper vessels (most likely for drinking), and fine clothing. Since camels were the most common means of transporting both people and goods in Arabia, rulers preferred horses and mules. Foreign traders could find many varieties of frankincense and myrrh, including resins from both cultivated and wild trees. In Muza, traders could also buy alabaster, which was used to make perfume bottles.

The author of the *Periplus* calls the coastal region of southwestern Arabia (modern Yemen) the "Frankincense Country."[23] The mountainous terrain and the climate were harsh, but people made terraces for their crops and developed irrigation to cultivate frankincense. Modern archaeological surveys of the region reveal terraces and palaces built of imported marble.[24] However, working conditions in the land of frankincense must have been terrible. The author of the *Periplus* says: "The frankincense is handled by royal slaves and convicts. For the districts are terribly unhealthy, harmful to those sailing by and absolutely fatal to those working there—who, moreover, die off easily because of the lack of nourishment."[25] The criminals were probably local, but the slaves most likely came from Africa.

The infrastructure for the frankincense trade stretched all the way across the peninsula to the mouth of the Persian Gulf. The coastal region east of Yemen (in modern Oman) also had direct shipping routes to India. Traders frequented the Indian port of Barygaza, where they acquired copper, sandalwood, teak, and ebony. Persian Gulf pearls were exported from Oman to more northern parts of the Arabian Peninsula and to Barygaza. However, the *Periplus* says that "both ports of trade export to Barygaza and Arabia pearls in quantity but inferior [in quality] to the Indian."[26] Indian pearls, especially those from the strait between southern India and Sri Lanka, were of the highest quality. Loaded with goods from the Arabian Peninsula and the Persian Gulf, in addition to the commodities from the Mediterranean, Roman ships were then ready to proceed to India, where they would trade these goods for pearls and other Indian products, as well as Chinese silks.

Barygaza was the most important Indian port for the Red Sea-based traders who plied the Arabian Sea, but it was not the first Indian port on their itinerary. That port was Barbaricum, at the mouth of the Indus River, which offered goods from India, Central Asia, and even further afield.[27] Around 50 CE, the Kushans—descended, as mentioned, from the Yuezhi nomads who had established themselves in Bactria— were crossing the Hindu Kush Mountains and occupying large parts of northern India. Their regime embraced many different ethnic groups, including Parthians and Sakas, both nomadic groups that had migrated to South Asia just ahead of the Kushans. "Saka" was the Asian name for Scythians. A few years later, the *Periplus* refers to this region as under the control of the Scythians. According to the *Periplus*, all foreign goods that came into this port had first to be transported up the Indus to a metropolis ruled by a king. This king was probably one of the Kushan rulers, because in this region the Scythians had become subjects of the Kushans. The Kushans were key players in the creation and subsequent control of the Silk Road trade, and many Chinese, Central Asian, and Himalayan goods under the direct control of the Kushans were available in Barbaricum.

The Romans used costus, bdellium, lyceum, and nard as spices, dyes, and medicines, and all came from plants grown in the high mountains of Kashmir and in the Himalayas. Turquoise, a light blue stone from Khurasan, in the northeast part of Iran, and lapis lazuli, a dark blue stone from Badakshan in northeast Afghanistan, were also in demand. Although these two stones have been considered semiprecious in modern times, both of them, and especially lapis lazuli, were very valuable at the time the *Periplus* was written. All of these were products found in the Kushan Empire.

The markets of Barbaricum were also filled with valuable goods from outside the Kushan domain. According to the *Periplus*, one such item was the "Seric [Chinese] pelt." Since furs were not a Chinese product, and the furs used in China generally came from peoples who lived on the steppe lands north of China, these furs, including sable and other precious kinds, were most likely from the cold areas north of Central Asia and China. Another product available at Barbaricum that came from outside the Kushan-controlled territories was silk yarn. At this time, all silk yarn came from China, and at Barbaricum the Romans bought this yarn instead of silk textiles. The Romans had already started weaving textiles out of imported silk materials for their own market. In the eyes of the Roman traders, the most important Indian products at Barbaricum included cotton cloth and indigo, a blue dye popular for textiles in the ancient world.

The Roman traders paid for these products with a variety of goods, including coral and the yellow gemstone topaz, both from the Red Sea region. They also paid with frankincense and other aromatic materials from the Arab countries, which they had obtained en route to India, and the glass vessels, silver and gold plates, and wine that they had loaded on their ships in the Mediterranean. However, Barbaricum was not the most important Indian port. After sailing through the dangerous waters around the Kathiawar Peninsula, a trader finally reached the Gulf of Cambay, where Barygaza was located.[28] Anchoring in the port of Barygaza was not easy, according to the *Periplus:*

> This gulf which leads to Barygaza, since it is narrow, is hard for vessels coming from seaward to manage.... At the very mouth of the gulf, there extends a rough and rock-strewn reef.... Opposite it, on the left-hand side, is [a] promontory...; mooring here is difficult because of the current around it and because the bottom, being rough and rocky, cuts the anchor cable. And, even if you mange the gulf itself, the very mouth of the river on which Barygaza stands is hard to find, because the land is low and nothing is clearly visible even from nearby. And, even if you find the mouth, it is hard to negotiate because of the shoals in the river around it. For this reason local fishermen in the king's service come out with crews and long ships...to meet vessels and guide them up to the Barygaza.[29]

Nevertheless, the journey to Barygaza was worthwhile. In addition to the goods available at Barbaricum, the Roman traders could also acquire highly desired tropical products, such as pepper and ivory. Here, too, were agate and carnelian, precious stones from the valley of the Narmada River, which linked the port to a vast hinterland in central and northern India. From the Narmada valley, a caravan would follow a land route to Ujjain, a flourishing commercial city in central India, then northward to Mathura, the southern capital of the Kushan Empire, on the bank of the Yamuna River, a tributary of the Ganges River. In addition, the routes from Mathura, the Kushan southern capital, to Gandhara (in what is now northern Pakistan), their northern political center, were well established.

Close commercial connections between the western coast and the northwestern region of India were already old at this time, having started in the time of the Seleucids around the third century BCE. In fact, ancient Greek coins, drachmas bearing Greek legends, were still in circulation in the market of Barygaza at the time of the *Periplus*. Barygaza received many visitors from Gandhara and Bactria. The *Periplus* claims that Gandharans and Pushkalavatians, both of whom were peoples of northwestern India, lived inland from the port. Pushkalavati was a large metropolis of the Kushan Empire (near modern Peshawar). "Above these is the very warlike nation of the Bactrians, who are under their own king," says the *Periplus*.[30] However, historians now know that some two hundred years earlier, the Greeks had lost control of Bactria (probably before the Kushans' arrival). When those Greek-speaking Roman traders saw Greek letters on coins circulated in the ports, either the older ones or the Kushan coins, they probably assumed that north Afghanistan was an independent Greek country. This reference to "Bactrians" in the *Periplus* most likely refers to the Kushans, who were by then at the apex of their military and commercial power, which included control over the ports the Romans frequented on India's western coast.

Thus the seafaring trade of the Roman Empire finally connected with the Central Asian Silk Road through the ports of Barygaza and Barbaricum. But the Roman traders did not stop there. Their ships traveled along the western coast of India, stopping at various ports for more tropical spices. And once they arrived at the tip of the Indian Peninsula, they found India's high-quality pearls. They even went around the cape and ventured along the eastern coast of the peninsula.[31] There, in the Bay of Bengal, they saw many different kinds of ships arriving, all the way from the mouth of the Ganges and from the peninsulas and islands of Southeast Asia. The author of the *Periplus* knew that silks from China were also available on the lower Ganges, but the voyage there was beyond the Romans' ability. On the southeast coast of the Indian peninsula, Roman traders landed at a port called Poduca, near modern Pondicherry, and built a trading depot. They built warehouses, workshops for processing merchandise, and docks for ships. The date of their establishment is roughly the mid-first century CE, around the time of the *Periplus*. According to a South Indian literary work of that time, "in different places of Puhār the onlooker's attention was arrested by the sight of abodes of [Romans], whose prosperity was never on the wane. On the harbor were to be seen sailors come from distant lands, but for all appearance they lived as one community."[32] Ships coming in from Southeast Asia on this coast were precursors of the Southeast Asian spice trade that would flourish many centuries later. The Romans gave up this trading depot after more than a century of occupation, probably due to market changes in their own homeland.

The *Periplus* makes no mention of Roman sailors going beyond Poduca. In territories controlled by the Roman Empire, the bulk of goods arriving from the East came via Central Asia. Caravan cities such as Palmyra were Roman trading depots dealing with traders from Persia. The sea route linking the Red Sea to the Arabian Sea reached Indian ports, primarily Barbaricum on the mouth of the Indus River and Barygaza on the Gulf of Cambay. The Roman traders had heard about the militant nomads ruling in the formerly Greek hinterland but did not know much about the people who controlled the sources of the goods they wanted. The Kushans, having established their power over the land routes from China to the western parts of India, took full advantage of the Roman maritime trade, as well as their old commercial ties to the Chinese, to build a regime crossing Central Asia and South Asia.

CHAPTER 3

The Kushan Empire and Buddhism

It is hard to believe that the Buddha, an austere ascetic, would advise people to accumulate wealth and make investments. But Buddhists traders during the time of the Kushans heeded this advice from him:

> Whoso is virtuous and intelligent,
> Shines like fire that blazes.
> To him amassing wealth, like a roving bee
> Its honey gathering,
> Riches mount up as an ant-heap growing high.
> When the good layman wealth has so amassed
> Able is he to benefit his clan.
> In portions four let him divide that wealth.
> So binds he to himself life's friendly things.
> One portion let him spend and taste the fruit.
> His business to conduct let him take two.
> And portion four let him reserve and hoard;
> So there'll be wherewithal in times of need.[1]

By being good Buddhists, the Kushans, who had built an empire that crossed Central Asia and South Asia, came to control a strategic portion of the Silk Road. Originally nomads on the Eurasian steppe, they had become rulers of a sedentary society who benefited from the long-distance trade passing through their territory. Their patronage of Buddhist institutions enabled them to flourish as a commercial power. Buddhist institutions in India, under the patronage of these foreign rulers, also benefited from the trade. With wealth flowing into their monasteries, Buddhists modified their theology and expanded their organizations to create a world religion. From the mid-first century to the mid-third century CE, when the Kushans controlled the main stream of trade, Buddhism spread to China and other Asian countries via the Silk Road.

Ruling a sedentary society with enormous cultural diversity was a challenge the Kushans met very well. Handling the international trade that converged on their domain required them to learn how to read and write many different languages and scripts and to accommodate many different religious practices. The urban economy flourished with the commercial traffic. Not only were palaces in big cities built with sturdy baked bricks, so were modest dwellings in small towns. Roads linked prosperous cities to ports and frontier towns.

How did the Kushans transform themselves from nomadic conquerors into the successful rulers of a diverse sedentary society? Unfortunately, there is not much in the way of written records to tell us. When they first settled in Bactria, the Kushans had no script to record their stories or transactions, and they never produced a great historian. Thus, to find out how they administered the country and managed the trade, scholars have searched out scattered data in Chinese, Sanskrit, Greek, and Latin and deciphered words on Kushan coins and inscriptions on the remains of temples and monasteries.

These fragmentary sources reveal that the Kushan kings relied on existing local institutions, such as caste hierarchies, traders' guilds, and religious organizations, to manage daily affairs. They also adopted parts of the political and cultural legacies of former rulers of the regions they now dominated, including the Persians, Greeks, Parthians, and Sakas. They never built a typical agricultural empire, with a strong bureaucracy to control every aspect of life. Their administration did not even reach the village level to collect a tax from farmers. The Kushans brought with them the beliefs and social structures forged from centuries of living on the steppe, and they mixed many of those customs in with the sedentary life of Hellenistic Bactria. After the Kushan army crossed the Hindu Kush Mountains, the regime also embraced Indian beliefs and practices, including those of the Brahmanical Hindus, Jains, and—most important by far—Buddhists. The flourishing commerce in the Kushan-held areas of northwestern India attracted many believers from the eastern Gangetic plain, as well as some other parts of India. The Kushans synthesized diverse practices into a unique state that became the economic as well as the cultural center of South and Central Asia for at least two hundred years.

For millennia, people on the steppe had practiced ancestor worship and had believed in the supreme power of heaven. The Kushan kings, long before they came to Bactria, called themselves "Son of Heaven" or "Son of God." Ritual occasions such as the inauguration of a chief or engagement in war called for a sacrifice to heaven. The Yuezhi, Saka, and other nomads who migrated to Bactria and further south and west most likely shared similar beliefs about the power emanating from this heaven. The Kushans kept this basic religious tenet from the steppe. Nevertheless, their unification of diverse groups, mainly the Yuezhi and most likely the Sakas and Parthians, marked a transition from a nomadic tribal system to a state based on territory and agricultural production.

The Kushan kings retained their steppe-style robes and trousers, which sustained their prestige as horse-riding archers, to distinguish themselves from their subjects. In addition to successfully ruling a sedentary society, they patronized the diverse religions that had already found a home in the region. The Kushans were not the first foreign rulers of this land, and their predecessors had also brought their religions with them. The Persian Empire included Bactria from the late sixth century to the fourth century BCE and left in its wake both Zoroastrian fire altars and cults from other parts of the empire, such as the goddess Nana from Mesopotamia. Alexander's campaign brought new gods and did not suppress those that had come before them; the Greek pantheon was inclusive and open. The Hellenistic states of the Seleucids and the Bactrians maintained the Persian and Mesopotamian cults, gods, and shrines. On the southern bank of the Amu River, in the ruins of the Greek city Ai Khanoum, all the major shrines archaeologists have located so far are of Middle Eastern origin.[2]

Greek gods, such as Hercules and Aphrodite, had long been popular in Bactria. A giant marble foot wearing a Greek-style sandal has been found in one of the shrines in Ai-Khanoum. Although it is remotely possible that it belonged to a supreme god of another religion, this foot most likely belonged to a huge marble statue representing Zeus. In general, the shrines and idols in this Greek city on the Oxus look very much like the religious remains in the caravan cities such as Palmyra. The Hellenistic regimes in Afghanistan and the Indo-Greek states east of the Hindu Kush Mountains had also been familiar with South Asian traditions, especially Buddhism. Indeed, the Greek king Menander was hailed in Buddhist tradition as a great patron of Buddhism.

By the time the Yuezhi arrived at Ai Khanoum, it was most likely in the hands of other nomads who had taken it from the Greeks. The conquerors would have captured a city such as Ai Khanoum only after a long siege, most likely killing many defenders and looting the palace and even some of the temples. But it is clear that the Yuezhi, who were shrewd and affluent steppe traders, appreciated the Greek city's marble temples supported by Corinthian columns and also realized that it was in their own interests not to attack its numerous established gods. They also seem to have appreciated the grandeur of the Hellenistic palace, which was far more impressive, if not more comfortable, than their

Merchants probably used this three-inch-tall bronze bust of Athena as a scale weight in the Roman-Indian trade. It was found, along with several similarly sized bronze statues, in a treasury that dates to Kushan times, in Begram, Afghanistan. The workmanship shows it was made in Hellenistic Egypt, probably Alexandria, in the Roman Empire. Erich Lessing / Art Resource, NY

tents. Under these circumstances, the Yuezhi-Kushans began to exert control over the formerly Hellenistic land.

The first thing to do, of course, was to establish order and collect taxes. When the Chinese envoy Zhang Qian visited the Kushan camps around 128 BCE, before the Yuezhi entered Bactria, there was no supreme king, but numerous Greek-style city-states ruled by their own sovereigns.[3] The Hellenized population had continued to maintain theaters, gymnasiums, and worship of city gods or goddesses. The Kushans probably left these cities alone, and even paid homage to their gods to win the support of the locals. The peoples who had lived in Bactria before the Greeks had also retained their own languages and cultures, as did nomadic groups who had arrived before and after the Yuezhi.

The Kushans' new state adopted the administrative system the Persian Empire had used to rule the region several hundred years earlier, which Parthian and then Saka rulers had handed down. To control each conquered territory remote from the imperial center, the Persians had employed a satrap, a governor with great autonomy and authority. His obligation was to maintain order and pay a regular tribute to the center. The Kushans named their governors *ksatrapas* and *mahaksatrapas*, both Sanskrit versions of the Persian word for "satrap." The first term is a direct translation; the second has, in addition, the Sanskrit prefix *maha-*, "great." The Kushans used Sanskrit titles because the largest population of the region including Bactria spoke several vernacular dialects of Sanskrit, the language of India's orthodox Brahmanical culture.

The region of Gandhara, southeast of the Hindu Kush, had a similar demographic and cultural composition. In the mid-first century CE, the Kushans extended their power over such Hellenistic cities as Pushkalavati and the city across the Indus River to Pushkalavati's east: Taxila. Farther south, especially in the Yamuna River region, where the Kushans established their southern capital Mathura, Hellenistic influence was less obvious. Mathura was the birthplace of the Vasudeva-Krishna cult of Hinduism, a center of Jainism, and a territory where Buddhism had begun to flourish.

As foreign rulers, Kushan kings and ksatrapas needed to remind their South Asian subjects of their divine origin. To do so, Kushan kings built *devakula*, literally "temples of the divine family." Archaeologists have uncovered two such temples, one in Mat, a village near Mathura, and another at Surkh Kotal, an archaeological site in Afghanistan. Inscriptions dated to the Kushan period mention more royal family temples. Both of those discovered so far contain larger-than-life-size statues of Kushan kings. The statue of the great king Kanishka in Surkh Kotal is almost identical to the one in Mat. The archaeologists who excavated the sites could not determine what deity was actually worshiped in these temples.[4] The statues of the kings may have been either idols or images of patrons of a main deity from the Middle East, Greece, or India. Either way, the devakula symbolized the divine nature of the ruling lineage.

In Bactria, Gandhara, and Mathura, Kushan rulers used both Greek letters and the Kharoshthi script (an evolution of the Aramaic script that the Persians had brought to India) to write the various Sanskrit dialects. The inscriptions in the temple of Surkh Kotal are written in Greek letters, and those in Mat are in a Kharoshthi script. Whereas in Bactria and Gandhara the Greek alphabet was popular, Kharoshthi and Brahmi, another Indian script, were prevalent in the territory surrounding Mathura. Without a written language on the steppe, the Yuezhi-Kushan conquerors adopted the scripts of conquered peoples in order to build an efficient government, maintain a successful tax system, record commercial transactions, and proclaim their own divinity on temple walls.

By the first century CE, the Silk Road trade had created connections from China to the Mediterranean Sea. The international trade passing through the Kushans' territory was quite different in nature from the early horse–silk bartering on the borders of China. The Kushans began to issue coins that both displayed their authority and facilitated the trade. The coins of previous rulers that were already circulating in the markets when the Kushans first arrived in Bactria were inscribed with words in either the Greek alphabet or the Kharoshthi script, regardless of the native tongue of the authority issuing the coins. The Greek authorities in Bactria had issued the best-quality coins of the time, even better than those found in the cities of Greece. On the earliest of these Greek coins, the inscriptions were exclusively in Greek. The profile of the king is well executed on the faces of these coins, and on their backs they often have images of Greek deities. During the second century BCE, this changed: Kharoshthi script was added to the Greek, and Middle Eastern or Indian gods were depicted on the back. Thereafter, the Parthians, Sakas, and Kushans all used both Greek and Kharoshthi.

In order to accommodate one of their major trading partners, the Romans, the Kushans based their coins on the aureus, a Roman gold coin. The Kushan gold, silver, and copper coins bore images of the Kushan kings and numerous deities, including the Sumerian goddess Nana, the Persian gods Oado and Atash, the Hindu gods Vasudeva and Siva, and, of course, the Buddha. The titles of the Kushan kings, inscribed on the coins in various languages, were "King of Kings," "Great King," and "Son of Heaven." The equivalent of the word "king" appears in Greek (basileus), Persian (shah), or the northwest dialect of Sanskrit (rao). A coin found in a Buddhist stupa near Jalalabad in modern Pakistan illustrates Kushan cosmopolitanism. On the face of the coin is a likeness of King Kanishka and the inscription "Raonanorao Kanirki Korno" in the Greek alphabet, representing words in the northwest dialect of Sanskrit that meant "King of Kings, Kanishka, of Kushana." On the reverse side of the coin is an image of the Buddha with a halo. It is one of the earliest surviving images of the Buddha. He is wearing a knee-length robe similar to that worn by the king. Just like the king on the face of the coin,

The legend on the gold coin of King Kanishka says "King of Kings, Kanishka, of Kushana." The message is recorded in a language local to the northwestern region of South Asia but is written with the Greek alphabet. Greek legacy persisted there long after Hellenistic states disappeared from the region. Image copyright © The Metropolitan Museum of Art / Art Resource, NY

the Buddha stands with feet pointing outward, a typical posture of the steppe people who spent so much time on horseback. There is a Kushan royal emblem next to the Buddha's left hand, and on his right there is an inscription in Greek letters meaning "the Buddha."

Multicultural coins and the Kushans' cosmopolitan attitude facilitated the trade that passed through their territory, which had access to both land routes passing through the Parthian Empire and sea routes that linked the ports of western India to ports further west that provided land portages to the Mediterranean. The Kushans also controlled both the steppe and oasis routes of the Central Asian Silk Road. Both the rulers and traders of the Kushan Empire profited from the trade and enjoyed goods from all over Eurasia. Archaeologists have uncovered a great treasury in the palace building at Kapisi (present-day Begram), a town in Afghanistan that served as the summer capital of the Kushan kings. Like later British rulers who could not stand the midsummer heat on the Indian plain in their European suits, the Kushan kings, with their steppe-style boots and robes, found refuge in the cool mountain area. The treasury, with the accumulated riches of 150 years, contained a wide variety of exotic wares, including bronze sculptures from the Mediterranean, Indian ivory carvings, and lacquer ware from China.[5] The only thing "missing" in this collection is silk. Given the poor state of preservation of the other goods, it must have simply disintegrated over the centuries.

The Kushan ruling elite led a luxurious life. They lived in palaces built in Hellenistic, Persian, or Indian architectural styles, rode around on horseback during their leisure time, visited and made donations to various shrines, and also gathered together to enjoy grape wine. This luxurious lifestyle even extends to the religious art—particularly Buddhist—produced under Kushan patronage. Greek, Roman, steppe, and Indian traditions are all obvious in these artworks. In the ruins of a Buddhist monument near Swat in Pakistan, archaeologists have found a series of sixteen carved stone panels that made up the risers of a staircase leading to the main stupa, a tower containing the relics of the Buddha. Corinthian columns with acanthus capitals suggest that the figures are actors in a Greek-style theater. On one panel, three men are playing musical instruments while another three are clapping their hands in time. One of the men is playing a harp, a Greek instrument. Another is playing a drum and a third an unidentifiable musical instrument. They are wearing belted tunics, somewhat Roman in style, but their trousers look like those of the horsemen of the steppe. Their conical hats, a signature of the early nomads, seem to be made of animal hide. So what are we looking at? A Kushan group wearing Roman clothing and playing Greek music?

The figures in another panel look more like Mediterranean peoples. Like Greeks, they wear tunics, but they are wearing boots instead of sandals. The woman in the center is dressed primly in the Greek style, while another woman is focused on her drinking, letting her body drapery fall off shoulder. A man holding a beaker appears to be her waiter. Another figure carries what is probably a wineskin made of a whole sheepskin. Another "waiter" carries a krater, a large Greek-style wine bowl.

In a third panel, the grapes one figure holds indicate that the wine in the scene is grape wine. He wears a robe in the Gandharan style, which had evolved from the toga, but also a pair of trousers that link him to steppe cultures. The other four feasting figures in the panel wear little. The figures on a fourth panel look Indic, and their lower bodies are covered with something resembling a modern-day dhoti or loincloth. Four of them are holding lotus flowers and look very pious. Figures in Mediterranean-style clothing on a fifth panel are again very cheerful, enjoying the music and the drinking.

This group of sculptures poses interesting questions for theologians and historians of Buddhism. What stories were the panels telling, and what messages were they conveying to the worshipers and pilgrims who came to this Buddhist shrine? They may represent scenes from a drama, which became a useful means of preaching and proselytizing for Buddhists in Kushan times. A Buddhist scholar closely associated with the Kushans, Ashvaghosha, wrote several plays with Buddhist themes, and fragments have survived in a Central Asian oasis. The pilgrims who visited the site during Kushan times probably knew the stories depicted in the scenes. Scholars haven't been able to decode the stories, but they can tell that these artistic representations reflect the real life of that time. In sites at various seaports, archaeologists have found shards of Roman amphorae, some with a residue of wine. In the city of Taxila in the Gandharan region, excavators have found ceramic, bronze, and silver drinking vessels, all made in Greco-Roman styles.[6] In Buddhist monasteries at Shaikhan Dheri, a site in the Gandharan region, archaeologists have found many wine storage jars and distillation equipment.[7] It is a puzzling find, suggesting that Buddhist monasteries were producing liquor, even though such activities were contrary to their centuries-old monastic discipline.

Human figures on Gandharan sculptures often look Greek or Roman, but those in Mathura, Sangol, and other Buddhist sites in central India look Indian. On a Buddhist stupa made with red sandstone from Mathura, a group of beautiful girls in a vineyard dance around kraters of wine on the ground. Either they wear short skirts or their bodies are simply wrapped with a piece of thin cloth. The textiles look so thin and fine that one assumes the artist meant to depict silk. While musicians play in the background, a group of dwarfs, beneath the main figures, ladle wine from a krater and frolic with each other. The drinking and dancing are obviously Hellenistic, but the faces and figures of the dancers and musicians appear more Indian than Greek.

Again it might seem difficult to make out the Buddhist context of this work of art. But as Buddhist institutions benefited from the economic prosperity of northwestern and western India, they became part of the region's lively urban cultural life. And it was from there that Buddhism developed into the most powerful religion of India and Asia east of Iran. Kushan cosmopolitanism prepared Buddhists to proselytize in diverse societies. At the same time, dramatic transformations within Indian Buddhist institutions and theology made the religion distinctly different from what it had been during its early days on the Lower Ganges Plain.

In the sixth and fifth centuries BCE, the Buddha had explained that life is full of suffering; all this suffering is caused by desire, and only the termination of desire can end suffering. One should therefore follow the right approaches in order to achieve the termination of suffering and reach the state of *nirvana: nir* means "none," and *vana* means "state of existence." The Buddha proposed a set of disciplinary methods called the "Eight Right Approaches" for his disciples and lay followers, who were financial supporters of his school of thinking.

The teachings of the Buddha were simple and logical. There was no need for intervention from supernatural powers, and there was no room for miracles. In this period of social, political, and economic upheaval, the numbers of the Buddha's followers in India grew quickly and the new teachings took root in many cities on the Gangetic plain. However, this Buddhism faced a serious obstacle to its spread to other lands: Asians outside Indian culture could not grasp the concept of nirvana, which was based on the uniquely Indic concept of rebirth. (A creature is reborn into another after its death, so that the suffering starts again. Only through nirvana would the endless suffering cease.) Why would people want to be in a state of "nonexistence"? For peoples outside the Indic culture who did not believe in rebirth, the concept of nirvana was puzzling.

The Buddha and his disciples led simple lives, wandering from town to town to preach while begging for food. They were satisfied with one meal a day and never had a permanent residence. The Buddha actually died on the road. But this simple lifestyle was hard to maintain without the support of a stable group of lay believers. and the Buddha and his disciples could not till the land, because tilling killed insects and the act of killing would cause more suffering in one's future lives. Someone else had to do the dirty work to feed them. As the Buddha's disciples increased in number, they organized themselves into a *sangha*, literally "gathering" or "congregation." Once the number in a sangha reached a few hundred monks, only the great cities could afford to receive the Buddha and his disciples, and only prosperous traders could afford to feed them. Meanwhile, the patronage of Buddhist sanghas brought prestige to the urban residents in an agriculture-based society. The Buddha himself advised merchants to accumulate wealth by making investments and working diligently like bees so that the Buddhist sangha could gain sufficient financial support from lay believers. The creation of wealth was not only beneficial to society but also brought religious merit to the donor. This mutual dependence produced a natural alliance between the commercial communities and the Buddhist sangha.

This relationship was crucial to the expansion of the religious order of Buddhism to areas outside India during the Kushan period. The international trade and urban prosperity under the Kushans drew the center of Buddhist activities to the west and northwest of the Indian subcontinent during the first and second centuries CE. During the Kushan period, stupas, or monuments containing the relics of the Buddha, as well as pilgrimage sites commemorating the Buddha's life sprang up in Mathura and Gandhara. Statues of the Buddha were erected and became idols for worship. Yet in the early Buddhist texts, the Buddha was only a sage, an enlightened one, who had vanished into the realm of nirvana and left behind his teachings to guide his disciples. He was not a god and therefore was not worshiped in the form of an idol. A significant development in Buddhist theology between the fifth century BCE and the first century CE underlay this dramatic change in religious practice.

For merchants from outside India to understand Buddhism, Buddha needed to be a god, and piety had to bring more tangible benefits than nirvana. During the Kushan period, around the first couple of centuries CE, a new text, the *Sadharmapundarika*, or the *Lotus Sutra*, prescribed a way for ordinary followers to achieve salvation:

> 83. Others, who had images of [Buddhas] made of the seven
>   precious substances, of copper or brass, have all of them reached
>   enlightenment....
> 88. Those who offered flowers and perfumes to the relics of the
>   [Buddhas], to Stūpas, a mound of earth, images of clay or drawn on
>   a wall;
> 89. Who caused musical instruments, drums, conch trumpets, and noisy
>   great drums to be played, and raised the rattle of cymbals at such
>   places in order to celebrate the highest enlightenment;
> 90. Who caused sweet lutes, cymbals, tabors, small drums, reed-
>   pipes, flutes of—or sugarcane to be made, have all them reached
>   enlightenment.[8]

By making donations to Buddhist monasteries, believers could rest assured that they would be carried across the ocean of sufferings in the *mahayana* ("great vehicle").[9] The rise of the Mahayana school of Buddhism during the Kushan period changed the direction of Buddhist development. In theory, Mahayana Buddhism emphasized the elusiveness of physical reality, including material wealth. It emphasized the doctrine of eliminating material desire to an extent that many followers found hard to understand. Traders, accustomed to material transactions, easily grasped the idea of making payments for religious merits. During a time when the society was unprecedentedly rich, this new approach encouraged them and other wealthy urbanites to make very generous donations. Newly affluent Buddhist monasteries came to possess many material things, including grandiose stupas and monastic buildings.

To bridge the gap between the doctrine of self-denial and the materialism of the time, Mahayana Buddhism introduced a host of new deities as intermediaries. Known as bodhisattvas, they were people who had already merited nirvana but decided to stay outside its threshold in order to help others to cross the ocean of suffering. Among the numerous bodhisattvas, Avalokiteshvara, the hero of the *Lotus Sutra*, stands out in Mahayana history. He was said to be the most approachable bodhisattva and one who would go out of his way to help anyone in trouble, such as traders on a sinking ship plying the ocean or caravans threatened by robbers in a desert. Worshiping him with material wealth was even more rewarding than worshiping the Buddha, who remained immune to its allure.

Maitreya, Amitabha, and most other bodhisattvas had their own paradises to accommodate worshipers who were not yet ready for nirvana. They could stay in one of these paradises while waiting to be reborn into this world. The "Western Pure Land" of Amitabha was the most welcoming to Mahayana Buddhist followers, since Amitabha promised that whoever invoked his name when facing death, no matter what he had done in his lifetime, could be rescued and transported to his paradise. Amitabha's Western Pure Land, like other heavens and bodhisattvas' lands in the Mahayana belief system, was pleasantly decorated with silks and the "Seven Treasures": the various jewels listed in the inventories of merchants of that time.

The bodhisattvas replaced the old, monotonous, cyclical scheme of perpetual rebirth with a scheme that was totally new and colorful. The Mahayana vision of future lives was no doubt much more attractive to the pragmatically inclined. Rebirth into a beautiful heaven was much more desirable than reaching nirvana. For merchants, making donations was a much more satisfying and practical approach than self-denial. The gifts given in the name of the Buddha or bodhisattvas became the property of Buddhist monasteries. Wealthy monasteries used the donations to build stupas decorated with the Seven Treasures and temples decorated with sculptures. Because these Buddhist monasteries and monuments were so beautiful, evoking the paradises of the bodhisattvas, they attracted even more worshipers and donors.

The material wealth described by Mahayana Buddhist texts reflects the actual conditions of monasteries at that time. No longer wandering around, begging for their daily food, Buddhist monks settled in permanent residences. Large begging bowls carved in stone were set at the gate of the monasteries. The donations were no longer cooked rice or bread but gold or silver coins and valuables. Buddhist texts such as the *Lotus*

Sutra and the *Western Pure Land Sutra* specify the kinds of jewels Buddhist followers should donate to the Buddha and bodhisattvas according to the concept of the Seven Treasures.[10] The lists of the Seven Treasures vary in different texts, but they all include gold, silver, lapis lazuli, crystal, pearls, red coral, and perhaps emeralds or some other greenish stones.

With tremendous wealth in their hands, Buddhist monasteries became large economic enterprises, engaging in all kinds of business, including trading, investing, and the making of alcohol. The most important activity became building, maintaining, and expanding monasteries in order to promote Buddhism. The artistic achievements of Buddhist artists were unsurpassed. To make a monastery look like a paradise, the monks festooned stupas and buildings with silk and gems. The kinds of gems and silks encountered in the international trade along the Silk Road appear frequently in Mahayana Buddhist texts and were displayed on those monuments. In the Western Pure Land, "there are some trees of two gems, viz. gold and silver. There are some of three gems, viz. gold, silver, and beryl.... There are some of seven gems, viz. gold, silver, beryl, crystal, coral, red pearls, and diamonds as the seventh."[11] To illustrate the beauty of Buddhist heavens and to make their monasteries as beautiful as those heavens, Buddhist writers and priests strove to produce the most splendid combinations of colors as well as the most impressive displays of gems. The very commodities traded along the Silk Road came to characterize Buddhist art. Gold and silver represented not only their values in trade but also the colors yellow and silver. Crystal was treasured all the way from Rome to Han China, but the best specimens came from India. Red coral from the eastern Mediterranean is in the inventory of the *Periplus,* and at some archaeological sites other red stones were used in its place. Pearls, either from the Persian Gulf or southern India, were mostly white, but there were also red pearls. Multicolored stones, such as striped agate, cat's eye, opal, or carnelian were also necessary. The overall visual effect was supposed to be shiny, with a combination of golden yellow, silver, lapis blue, transparent crystal, red, green, and an iridescent quality. In this combination, the lapis lazuli blue stood out as the most striking and valued color. The ancient world valued lapis lazuli much more highly than people do today, and at that time its only major source, Badakshan in Afghanistan, was under the control of the Kushans. In the centuries that followed, in murals and statues of the Buddha, the hair of the Buddha took on a blue color, and celestial beings were depicted using lapis lazuli blue. In fact, lapis lazuli blue became the most characteristic color of Buddhist art wherever it spread.

Surrounded by a pavement of glass tiles, the stupa at Dharmarajika monastery in Taxila displays these splendid colors. When archaeologists excavated the site, they found fragments of various gems scattered around the monastic buildings.[12] Buddhist texts mention that incense made from frankincense and other fragrances was used during monastic services. Imagine a pilgrim walking into one of the Kushan monasteries: the faint smoke and fragrant smell of incense would make him feel like he was entering another world, apart from the urban noise and foul smells. Around the stupa and the railings, he would see colorful silk banners or festoons fluttering in the wind and the Seven Treasures, sewn onto flags or strung on sculptures, sparkling under the sun. Walking around the clean and transparent glass pavement and up the stairs, he would try to discern the meaning of the sculptures while appreciating the beauty of the artworks.

At the same time that trade attracted Buddhism to the northwestern and western regions of south Asia and made monasteries rich, Mahayana Buddhist texts served to increase the value of silks, incense, and gems. When monasteries grew into large institutions, they provided hospitality to traveling traders. Since the time of the Buddha, monks were accustomed to traveling along the trade routes in the company of merchants from city to city. They often took shelter during the rainy seasons, since the torrents of the South Asian monsoon greatly restricted travel. If the road was in a mountainous region, roadside caves were ideal. As monks and traders' caravans traveled the same routes year after year, they no doubt took shelter in the same caves season after season. In this way, the caves gradually became permanent places for worship and accommodations. In the first few centuries CE, when the Silk Road trade passed through India, hundreds and hundreds of Buddhist cave temples appeared on the northwestern part of the Deccan Plateau, along the routes linking the western Indian seaports to the core region of the Kushan Empire. When Mediterranean ships arrived at the western Indian coast, they anchored at Barygaza, Sopara, and Kalyana. From these ports, mountainous routes through the Deccan Plateau carried the cargo either north to Ujjain, Mathura, and Gandhara, or south to the Tamil country. As donations from traders enriched the cave monasteries, the natural caves along the routes were soon enlarged into cave temples and residences.

The Deccan region was never under direct Kushan control but was controlled by the West Ksatrapas, a polity created and managed by the Sakas, who had entered South Asia just ahead of the Kushans. However, an indigenous Deccan power, the Satavahanas, also took possession of

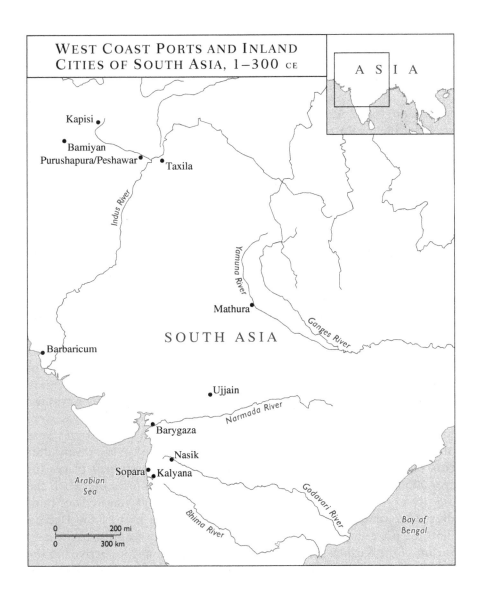

WEST COAST PORTS AND INLAND
CITIES OF SOUTH ASIA, 1–300 CE

ASIA

Kapisi

Bamiyan
Purushapura/Peshawar
Taxila

Indus River

Yamuna River

Mathura

Ganges River

SOUTH ASIA

Barbaricum

Ujjain

Narmada River

Barygaza

Nasik

Sopara Kalyana

Arabian
Sea

Godavari River

Bhima River

Bay of
Bengal

0   200 mi
0   300 km

the region from time to time. Still, the monks continued to excavate
their caves, and traders kept coming and going and even making deals
in them. Huge halls dug deep into the cliffs of the mountains, which
were often solid rock, became major cave shrines. Monks carved rock
into the shapes of wooden arches. In those early Buddhist caves of the

northwest Deccan, the center of worship was the stupa, a symbol of the Buddha's relics, which was also carved out of the rock. In the centuries that followed, all schools of Buddhism came to accept the Buddha's divinity, and images of the Buddha became objects of worship.[13]

Many donors recorded their donations by inscribing them on the walls, along with their names and titles. Some of these donors called themselves "Yavana," an Indian term for Greeks or Romans. The term here was used to refer to anyone from the northern shores of the Mediterranean. The Yavanas who made donations to Buddhist monasteries could have been Buddhist devotees, or perhaps they were just paying their respects to the religious institution that provided lodgings and a place for commercial dealings in a foreign country. Since Buddhism never required formal conversion or any ceremony to become a devotee, making a donation was meritorious enough to demonstrate one's devotion to the religion and to win the trust of the monastery. The Yavanas may well have been Roman traders who came to the ports by ship and ventured inland to pursue more business; they also could have been traders from the formerly Hellenistic states of northwestern India who came down to the ports to sell silks and furs in exchange for Roman goods.

There were also the names of traders who specialized in certain kinds of goods such as fragrances; local traders who called themselves "householders," a title for influential traders living in cities; and artisans belonging to the guilds of various professions. The wives, mothers, and other female relatives of these people often made their own donations to secure good fortune for their men on the road and make special wishes for their loved ones. Even traveling monks and nuns recorded their donations to the monasteries.[14] Monks and nuns continued to have their own incomes and savings even after joining a Buddhist sangha, it seems. The presence of Buddhist caves made the desolate mountain routes much more accessible for all.

Caves along the eastern coast of the Persian Gulf in southern Iran, specifically in Haidari and Chehelkhana, show a strong similarity to the inland Buddhist cave temple tradition.[15] Buddhist monks, along with the traders, may well have made efforts to propagate their faith in that direction, but if they did, there were no significant consequences in the Gulf. These cave temples, Buddhist or not, were soon abandoned.

Buddhism spread far more successfully along the northern land routes. Given the terrain, cave temples were not feasible in the plains around Mathura, or even in Gandhara. Afghanistan, however, had suitable terrain for excavating shrines and residences in caves. In addition to the many freestanding stupas and monasteries, cave shrines and monastic cells developed there in the early centuries CE. Buddhist cave temples featured images of both the Buddha and bodhisattvas. This type of cave sculpture continued to flourish long after the collapse of the Kushan regime and reached its apex in the fifth century CE. Destroyed by Taliban extremists in 2001, the gigantic standing Buddha carved in the rock mountain at Bamiyan, a valley in the Hindu Kush Mountains, exemplified this continuing tradition. Indeed, one might consider the monumental Buddha in Bamiyan as the starting point of the Central Asian Silk Road, which from Afghanistan to China was dotted with Buddhist cave shrines and monasteries.

In the first century CE, Buddhism began to spread out of the core areas of the Kushan Empire, by land routes that went from Afghanistan through other parts of Central Asia to China. Monks and their trader patrons brought with them Buddhist texts and built monasteries along the way. The texts also brought a new written language. In what was Gandhara (eastern Afghanistan and northern Pakistan), scholars have found a large quantity of Buddhist scrolls written in the Gandhari language—a Sanskrit dialect—with the Kharoshthi script.[16] Ghandari most likely was the daily language of the Kushans after they established their empire. From Gandhara, this script spread to east and north to various parts of Central Asia. In the centuries that followed, Kharoshthi became the main script in the Tarim Basin (now a part of China's Xinjiang Uighur Autonomous Region) for writing local languages.

The Kushan Empire ultimately fell to Iran's Sassanid Empire in the third century, but their script survived in the oases around the rim of the Takla Makan Desert. Scholars have long debated why this script prevailed. The Kharoshthi documents from the oases include administrative records, correspondence, and archives from Buddhist monasteries. Kushan refugees may have brought the script with them, or traders may have started the practice. The most important carriers of the script may well have been Buddhist institutions established in the oases.

The population in many oases was also growing, with new residents coming in from the steppe. Neither the original population nor the immigrants from the steppe had a written language before the coming of the Kharoshthi script. During the Han and thereafter, Chinese people used their native writing for administrative and diplomatic documents in the oases, but non-Chinese residents did not. Because the Chinese writing system does not spell out the sound of words, it cannot be used to write the sounds of other languages. In contrast, Kharoshthi was an alphabetic script that could be used to record the sounds of other languages and thereby transform them into written languages.

Languages spoken in the Tarim Basin (the larger geographic region that contains the Takla Makan Desert) in that period were mostly various dialects that had Indo-European roots. The Kharoshthi script fit well into the region's linguistic complexity. However, the variety of tongues has made deciphering the Kharoshthi documents of Central Asia exceedingly difficult for present-day scholars. While the Chinese language and script continued to be used for some official purposes, the Kharoshthi script was the writing system used for Buddhist texts and daily transactions. Sometimes both scripts appear on one medium. The coins found in Khotan, an oasis town on the southern rim of the Takla Makan Desert, have Chinese characters on one side and Kharoshthi letters on the other side.

The vast majority of the Kharoshthi documents are from the site of Niya, a town on the southern rim of the desert that had a huge Buddhist stupa at its center. The thousand or more fragments written in this script include documents in the form of wooden tablets, leather, silk textiles, and paper and legends inscribed on metal coins, while the Buddhist texts are on birch bark. These documents give a glimpse of the life of the Niya people and their role in trade. Silk textiles—not local products— were used as currency in the local trade, along with a variety of coins. Horses were a valuable commodity. The Buddhist monastery was an important political institution in the oasis. One Kharoshthi document from Niya is a record of the sale of a vineyard. The deal was apparently sealed in the Buddhist monastery, and several Buddhist monks were involved in the transaction as witnesses. Another document is a regulation for the local monastery; all the monk offenders were to pay their fines in bolts of silk textiles.[17] In addition to Kharoshthi documents, a number of Chinese documents written on wooden slips and silk textiles survive from the same site and the same period. All these thin slices of wood and pieces of inscribed silk have provided a wealth of information about the Chinese, the lost Indo-European languages, and life in ancient Niya. These records indicate that a vineyard was a salable commodity in Niya; thus, viticulture and winery must have been popular at the edge of desert. The monastery had much authority, if monks were witnesses in legal transactions. In addition, monks owned rolls of silk, and were disciplined by fines.

By the later third and early fourth century CE, China's imperial unity had dissipated, but Niya, as well as probably some other oasis states, remained under the suzerainty of the Western Jin, a successor state.

After a new wave of nomads flooded northern China, Central Asia, and Afghanistan in the fourth century, in the absence of any secular hegemony, Buddhist institutions began to take over control of the Silk Road. It would take another century or so for the most recently arrived nomads in China to establish themselves as patrons of the Silk Road.

Although Buddhism did not have a significant presence in Iran, Buddhist traders from Kushan territory maintained contacts with people in Iran by overland routes, and some early Buddhist converts in Iran even helped to spread Buddhism to China. Several of the earliest Buddhist preachers in China were actually Parthians from Iran. These early contacts between Iranian Buddhists and China most likely paved the way for other religions such as Nestorian Christianity and Manichaeism to travel from Iran to China along the Silk Road. Manichaeism emerged in Iran in the third century and spread both westward to the Mediterranean and eastward as far as China. The Manichaeism that spread to China shared similar iconographic forms and vocabulary with Buddhism. To some extent, Buddhist missionary efforts in Iran resulted in a Buddhist-styled Manichaeism, instead of a Buddhist institution in Iran.

During the Kushan era, Buddhist teachers—a group that included Parthians, Indians, and Kushans—established the Buddhist institution in China. In many cases, these teachers' countries of origin are obvious from their Chinese names. The Han Chinese, as well as their descendants for many centuries thereafter, liked to give Chinese names to foreigners, with surnames that were often abbreviations of the Chinese name for their countries of origin. Thus, in China, all Parthians shared the surname "An," after their dynastic name, Arsacid, and all the Kushans shared the surname "Zhi," which was taken from Yuezhi, the Chinese name for the confederation when it lived on the steppe. In the Later Han capital Luoyang, many traders and Buddhist priests with the surnames An and Zhi were active in propagating their faith. An Shigao, a priest who settled in Luoyang in 148 CE, was said to have been a prince in his own land who had given up his privileged life to preach Buddhism in China. An Shigao, together with another Parthian, the merchant An Xuan, initiated the systematic translation of Buddhist texts into Chinese. The early translations were poor in quality and only fragments survive. Some twenty years later, Zhi Loujiaqian, a Kushan monk, and Zhu Foshuo, an Indian, together with several Chinese collaborators, translated several important Mahayana Buddhist texts into Chinese.[18] Even so, it is quite likely that their translations circulated only within the city of Luoyang. Throughout the Han Dynasty, intellectual Buddhist activities in China do not seem to have engaged the

Chinese populace. All the foreign Buddhist preachers and traders in Han China—Parthians, Kushans, or Indians—were sponsored by Buddhist establishments located within the Kushan Empire.

Just as carved statues and decorated shrines had helped spread Buddhism in the Kushan Empire, they made it easier for people in foreign countries to understand and relate to the Buddhist teachings. Small Buddhist icons appeared all over Han China as aids to the Parthian, Kushan, and Indian teachers and their Chinese students who struggled over Sanskrit dialects and Chinese translations. Amateur Buddhist artists contributed sculptures depicting the Buddha's nirvana at a large-scale Buddhist shrine in a group of carvings on boulders in Kongwangshan, near Lianyungang, a coastal city now in Jiangsu Province near the Shandong border. Though the traces of the Buddha, in a supine position, are badly eroded, the figures surrounding him, mourning his departure, make the scene recognizable as a portrayal of his nirvana. Two small standing images of the Buddha are strikingly similar to the Buddha on a Kushan coin issued by Kanishka. Both on the coin and at Lianyungang he is shown wearing a knee-length, steppe-style robe and with his feet pointing outward. In other words, these are Kushan Buddhas. The worshipers also look like Kushans, with their conical hats and equestrian robes.

By which route and what means Kushan Buddhism reached this eastern edge of China is still debated. The lack of skill of the rock carvings indicates that the images probably were not intended for an established community but served a temporary need, such as a place of worship for those traveling outside their homeland. This shrine is nevertheless clear and definite evidence for the arrival of Buddhism—more specifically, Kushan Buddhism—in second-century China. The Kushan Empire and the Mahayana Buddhism it fostered were responsible for the landmarks on the various branches of the Silk Road that led from India to China.

CHAPTER 4

A Golden Age Emerges

Chinese silk appears frequently in the poems and dramas of Kalidasa (c. fifth century), an Indian playwright and poet who lived in the capital of the Gupta Empire at a time when the trade over the Silk Road made Chinese silk an available, though expensive, commodity in both Indian and Eurasian cities. As he wrote in *Kumarasambhara*, "the city appeared to be heaven itself transferred to another place, where *Mandara* flowers were strewn over the broad royal streets and where buntings and flags of Chinese silk flaunted in the air; and it appeared to be so by the blazing luster of the golden arches."[1] The fall of the Kushan Empire meant that no great power controlled the Central Asian Silk Road, yet large quantities of silk continued to pass through this region, thanks to autonomous trading networks sustained by religious institutions, merchants' organizations, and local communities. From the Mediterranean to China, traders found sources and supplied markets in spite of military hostilities, dynastic changes, and even imperial authorities' attempts to protect and pursue their own interests in silk by obstructing part of the trade.

The markets and products of the Han, Kushan, Parthian, and Roman empires may have created the Silk Road, but the trade and the cultural exchanges that resulted did not reach full maturity and splendor until after these empires had collapsed. Beginning in the early third century, they were in decline. Steppe nomads put pressure on the Han and Roman empires, while the Romans also had to contend with tribal peoples who lived in the forested areas to their north. Weakened by civil wars at the beginning of the third century, Han China was flooded with steppe nomads who changed the demographic character of China to a substantial degree. For more than a century, the Roman Empire *had* managed to fend off both the Germanic forest tribes to its north and Parthian and Sassanid Persians to the east, but the aftermath of these struggles weakened the Roman state considerably. Germanic tribes migrated into the Mediterranean area and intermingled with the local population, as had steppe nomads in China.

In the third century, the Sassanids had replaced the Parthians as the lords of the Persian Empire on the Iranian plateau and had quickly

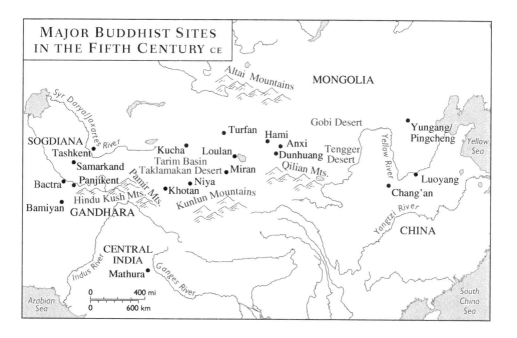

MAJOR BUDDHIST SITES
IN THE FIFTH CENTURY CE

embarked on a successful campaign against the Kushans. The Sassanids annexed the northern part of the Kushan Empire. Cut off from its access to the steppe, the southern part of Kushan Empire was taken over by India's newly rising Gupta Empire in the fourth century. These political changes produced a readjustment in the basic structure of the Silk Road trade. Government sponsorship and protection of the long-distance trade became unreliable or disappeared all together in some places. The Silk Road nevertheless survived and flourished amid the violence and chaos.

While these empires were falling apart, the oases on the desert routes continued to develop into towns and even major cities. The technology of digging deep wells and transferring water through canals enlarged the area suitable for cultivation. The oases could then support larger cities and more travelers than ever before. Buddhist cave shrines and statues continued to mark trade routes in both western India and Afghanistan. As already mentioned, the huge fourth- or fifth-century statues of the Buddha at Bamiyan in the Hindu Kush Mountains marked the western end of the Central Asian Silk Road. For many centuries the two statues, one thirty-seven meters (121 feet) and the other fifty-five meters (180 feet) tall, served as landmarks for travelers, Buddhist or not. When the Chinese pilgrim Xuanzang (600–664) passed through the Bamiyan valley during the early seventh century, he reported: "to the northeast of the king's city, carved in a mountain cliff, stands a rock statue of the Buddha about one hundred and forty to fifty *chi* in height, splendid with golden color and decorated with gems. To the east of statue there is a monastery, built by a previous king. East of the monastery stands a brass statue of the Buddha about a hundred *chi* tall."[2] Under the feet of these gigantic Buddha statues, a community of Buddhist monasteries would host travelers for centuries to come.

Around the same time or even earlier—around the fourth century—Buddhist caves had begun to appear at Kezil, an oasis on the northern edge of the Takla Makan Desert some forty miles west of Kucha; at Dunhuang, in the Hexi Corridor west of China's Yellow River; and at Yungang, in northern China's Shanxi Province. Several huge statues of the Buddha at Yungang, though less impressive than those at Bamiyan, dominated the entire group of caves, which stretch for more than one mile along its foothills. The Buddhist caves at Yungang mark the eastern end of the Silk Road of that time. From Bamiyan to Yungang, Buddhist monuments lined the entire length of the Central Asian Silk Road. Buddhist monasteries associated with the monuments provided the basic facilities for travelers. And by this time, this section of the Silk Road had developed into a relatively stable and viable commercial highway.

During the time that the gigantic standing statues of the Buddha bookended the road at Bamiyan and Yungang, the Hephthalites, also known as the White Huns, occupied the territory that had once been ruled by the Kushan Empire, having battled with the Gupta in central India. Meanwhile, many groups of nomads, including the Xianbei, entered northern China. The Hephthalites were not Buddhists, but they did not destroy any stupas or other sculptures. During the fourth and fifth centuries, the Bamiyan Buddhist complex developed under their rule. At the eastern end of the Silk Road, the Xianbei underwrote various Buddhist sculptures at Yungang.[3] Once the Xianbei consolidated their rule in the mid-fifth century as the Northern Wei Dynasty, the emperor had the five huge statues of the Buddha carved to assert himself and his ancestors as reincarnations of the Buddha.

As the huge Bamiyan and Yungang Buddhas were being carved, the initial construction of the Silk Road's Buddhist infrastructure was about to end. In Kucha, a region on the northern edge of the Takla Makan Desert, Buddhist caves had appeared as early as the end of the third century

Since the fifth century, the gigantic Buddha in Bamiyan beckoned exhausted travelers who had just crossed the Hindu Kush mountains from the north. The lush Bamiyan valley marked the South Asian terminus of the Central Asian Silk Road. Borromeo / Art Resource, NY

or the beginning of the fourth century. A complex of monasteries at the site of Kezil includes 236 caves. There are *chatya* (halls housing such things as stupas and images), preaching halls, and rooms for meditation and storage. The Mogao caves in Dunhuang, the Maijishan cave monastery, and the Binlingsi caves in the Hexi Corridor all appeared between the late fourth century and the early fifth century. The Mogao caves in Dunhuang were founded in 366 under a nomadic group called the Di. The monastery eventually developed into a large complex of about five hundred caves. Buddhist cave temples mushroomed while nomadic tribes occupied the area from Bamiyan to Yungang.

The cave shrines along the mountainous routes linking western Indian ports to the northern Indian plain continued to develop after the Kushan era. In the fourth and fifth centuries, mural paintings began to appear alongside the earlier rock reliefs and freestanding stone stupas and Buddhas in western Indian caves. The paintings in Ajanta and other western Indian cave temples soon became models of Buddhist mural art in Central Asia and China. The bodhisattvas were heavily decorated with gems, presumably the Seven Treasures given by devotees. At this time, Buddhist devotees preferred colorful pictures of their idols rather than bare stone sculptures. The Bamiyan Buddhas were covered with colorful painting. The statues at Yungang were also painted, but the colors have almost totally faded. Only the black pupils in the eyes of the Buddha retain their color. In the Mogao grottos at Dunhuang, not only the murals but also all the sculptures were colorful.

Buddhist artworks from India to Central Asia shared common themes. They were largely human figures. As images of the Buddha, bodhisattvas, and well-known disciples of the Buddha, they were the objects of worship. Donors and patrons who wanted to immortalize their contributions often had their own images carved or painted in the caves, unwittingly immortalizing period clothing and hairstyles for today's scholars. As do regional fashions, the architecture and vegetation portrayed in the paradises vary from region to region, but the flying figures of *apsarases* are always present. These demigods from Indian mythology sometimes fly with wings, like angels in Christian art, but more often they recline on long silk bands that float on the clouds—a symbol of their location far above the mere mortals on earth.

Some paintings represent stories of the former lives of the Buddha. These murals are difficult for many visitors to comprehend because they portray only a few scenes from long, involved stories. However, for the monks who meditated daily in the caves, a few scenes evoked the whole story. On one of the murals in a cave at Ajanta in western India, the depiction of the Buddha's large audience portrays various kinds of people, including horsemen wearing fur hats who obviously came from Central Asia. The scene reveals that in the fifth century, the western Indian section of the trade route was still well connected with Central Asia.

Central Asian Buddhist art did not, however, just imitate the Buddhist art of India. Other traditions, especially the Zoroastrian and later the Manichaean from Persia, mingled with the Buddhist art. Buddhist traders from Persia were a part of the vanguard who transplanted Buddhism to China, and their Zoroastrian background is apparent in the Buddhist art of the Silk Road. Fire worship, a symbol of Zoroastrianism, can be found even in early Buddhist sculptures. When the Sassanids took over Iran in the third century, they based their political legitimacy on a revival of ancient Achaemenid culture, including the Zoroastrian religion. The Sassanid revival was a success, and from the fifth century on, Zoroastrian traders brought their culture and way of life to the Silk Road.

Many of these Zoroastrian traders came from Sogdiana, a generally arid region flanked by the Amu and Syr rivers, both of which flow westward into the Aral Sea. Most of the population lived in oases towns. Ancient Sogdian cities such as Bukhara and Samarkand are still prosperous urban centers. After the fall of the Kushan Empire, the Sogdians became very prominent traders, and for more than a thousand years thereafter they would have a significant presence on the trade routes, mediating between nomads, oases dwellers, and sedentary empires. They, too, would leave their own cultural legacy on the Silk Road.

The early history of the Sogdians was similar to that of the Yuezhi; they were nomads and traders and formed agricultural communities. The early Sogdians, however, had closer relations with the Persians than with the Chinese. The Sogdians spoke an eastern dialect of the Persian language. A tablet in the palace of Darius in Susa mentions the Sogdians supplying lapis lazuli and carnelian to the Persian king, much as the Yuezhi had supplied jade to the Chinese rulers.[4] The Sogdians initially lived as nomads while engaged in trade, like the Yuezhi. Like the Yuezhi, some Sogdians settled down to farm and trade; others, as reported in the Chinese dynastic histories, continued their nomadic life until at least the fifth century CE. Unlike the Yuezhi, the Sogdians never established a great empire. During the post-Han period, Sogdian traders ventured into the markets of China, braving precarious political conditions. Sogdian letters found in a guard post on the Chinese frontier wall to the west of Dunhuang illustrate the risk those Sogdian traders had to take in order to conduct their lucrative businesses. In 313 CE, nomads flooded into northern China. In the letter, a merchant lamented the sack of Luoyang and Ye by nomads: "the last emperor, so they say, fled from Luoyang because of the famine and fire set to his palace and the city. . . . Luoyang is no more! Ye is no more!" The agents he sent to those places never returned or even sent back messages. He was afraid he would die soon and so sent this letter to his homeland to ask his relatives to distribute his property and protect his heir.[5] His letter never arrived, but it reveals to us the ancient Sogdian traders' daring commercial characters and lives.

From the fourth century on, Sogdian traders started to travel in the Indus Valley and leave their marks on the routes. Buddhist Sogdians looked for the sacred sites of the Buddha and worshiped on the road. On the steep cliffs on the banks of the Indus, they painted or scratched images of the Buddha and stupas so as to perform the rituals. They also inscribed their names and their wishes for protection of the Buddha at these sites of worship. Clusters of such Sogdian inscriptions remain on the rocks near an ancient river ford on the Indus, near Hunza.[6] This difficult route continues to serve as an artery of communication to the Indian subcontinent; a modern bridge links this ancient site to the modern Karakorum Highway, built by Pakistan as a transportation link with China. The Sogdians also gradually expanded their networks westward, and at least by the sixth century, their networks reached all the way to Europe.

From the early days of the Silk Road, the Sogdian language and script had been one of the main commercial languages. In the centuries after the collapse of the Han and Roman empires, the Sogdian language became more and more popular, and, after the sixth century, it became the most common language used among traders in Central Asia.

Many figurines buried in Chinese and Central Asian tombs from the period represent musicians, dancers, and other entertainers of Persian or Sogdian origin. Persian silk textiles were then considered high style in the markets of China, Central Asia, Byzantium, and even western Europe. The Sogdians carried prototypes of Sassanid silk textiles along the Silk Road, as well as in China proper, in Byzantine cathedrals, and in the churches of Europe. Among these prototypes were silk textiles with such motifs as two horses in confrontation, equestrian warriors, ducks, boars, and especially the *simurgh*, a creature with a mammalian head and the body of a bird. Some silk textiles were made in Iran, but design modifications betray the Central Asian, Chinese, and Byzantine origins of others.

After the collapse of the Roman and Han empires, Persia's Sassanid Dynasty became the superpower of Eurasia. Thousands of coins from Sassanid Persia have been found along the Silk Road and in neighboring lands. Sassanid coins, along with silk yarn and rolls of plain silk textiles, served as currency for international trade on the Silk Road. And even though the Arab Muslim conquest of Iran in the mid-seventh century abruptly stopped the issuing of Sassanid coins, the already existing ones continued to circulate for many years thereafter.

Gilded silver ware was another Persian specialty. Silver flasks, bowls, and plates were decorated with many of the same motifs used on Sassanid silk textiles, such as the simurgh, horsemen, and hunting scenes. The social and economic elite throughout much of Eurasia treasured these vessels and buried them in their tombs. As did silk textiles, the Persian technologies used to produce this silver ware soon spread to other countries. Tang Chinese artisans, probably with the aid of Persian specialists, were among those who soon began producing beautiful silver ware with Chinese motifs.

While the Persian artifacts and goods enjoyed a high demand among the items carried on the Silk Road, most dealers were probably not Iranians but Sogdians, particularly after the mid-seventh-century Arab conquest of Iran extinguished the Sassanid Empire. The homeland of the Sogdians (in and near modern-day Uzbekistan) remained largely independent for another hundred years or so.

Before the Sassanid conquest, many Sogdian traders had been Buddhists, but when the Sassanids took over Persia, most Sogdians became Zoroastrians or Manichaeans. Manichaeism had originated in Iran in the third century. It inherited the concept of dualism from Zoroastrianism. Manichaeism viewed the universe as the conflict of light and dark, goodness and evil. In the west, Manichaeism had absorbed the Gnostic tradition and borrowed the concept of salvation from Christianity. The rituals and icons of Manichaeism in the West were so similar to those of the Christians that Christians sometimes described Manichaeism as a Christian heresy. Meanwhile, in the East, Manichaeans borrowed iconic traditions from Buddhism and built many cave temples along the Central Asian trade routes, often right beside those of the Buddhists. The compositions of these murals are so similar to those of Buddhism that for decades scholars treated them as a kind of Buddhist art. When the Manichaeans ran into trouble with China's Tang Dynasty, the Chinese government accused them of pretending to be Buddhists in order to confuse people. Manichaean art, however, retained its special features, especially those expressing the doctrines of dualism and salvation.

While acting as the intermediaries between sedentary empires and nomadic confederations, the Sogdians spread their religions. Just as they had been among the earliest Buddhist preachers in China, Sogdians in the seventh and eighth centuries were preachers of Manichaeism. While acting as their commercial agents, the Sogdians converted the Uighurs, Turkish-speaking nomads, to Manichaeism. Thereafter, Manichaean temples and Uighur horse traders were always found together in Tang metropolitan areas.

The golden age of the cities in the Sogdian homeland lasted from the fifth to the eighth centuries, when rich traders enjoyed an opulent lifestyle and shared power with the sovereigns of the city-states. Just how opulent they were is revealed by murals in a rich eighth-century merchant's house in Panjikent, the site of a Sogdian city in modern Tajikistan. The house had a granary so large that its owner must have

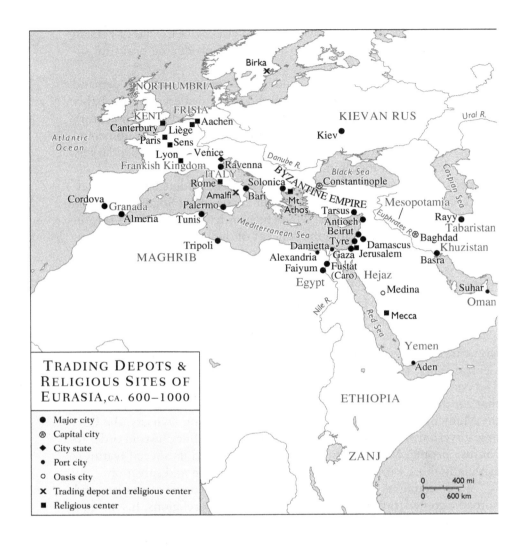

TRADING DEPOTS &
RELIGIOUS SITES OF
EURASIA, CA. 600–1000

- ● Major city
- ⊗ Capital city
- ◆ City state
- • Port city
- ○ Oasis city
- ✕ Trading depot and religious center
- ■ Religious center

been a grain dealer. The entire main hall of the house, including the ceiling, was lavishly painted. In this limited space, the owner reached for the level of grandeur of a royal palace.[7] On the southern wall, a divine couple sits on a luxurious, elongated throne. The arms and legs of the throne on the side of the male deity take the shape of a camel, while those on the side of the female deity form a ram. The throne appears to be covered with exquisite textiles that have Persian designs. In the left corner of the mural, a fire altar and various worshipers indicate the presence of the Zoroastrian tradition. The two figures on the throne could be patrons of the household as well as local gods.

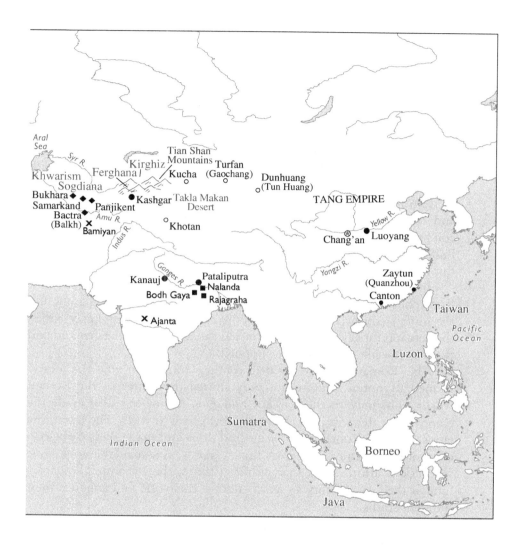

The wall at the northern end of the hall is divided into upper and lower sections. The upper section contains a painting of the ancient Mesopotamian goddess Nana, who had been popular within the Persian cultural sphere for many centuries, sitting on a lion. An image of the Buddha is painted in the lower section, above the door. A panorama of harvest festivities is depicted in the remaining part of the mural, along with the murals on both the east and west sides of the hall. Kings are shown receiving various sorts of tribute and acknowledging respect from both local and distant peoples. The fur hats, turbans, and designs on the clothing all give clues to the origins of these people and to fashion at that time. These fragmented murals in Panjikent preserve the last glimpse of the cosmopolitan life in the oasis towns and of the eclectic religious attitude of the Sogdian trading communities before the Islamic conquest.[8]

Among all the different religious traditions that existed in the oases of Central Asia, Buddhism remained the dominant religion on the Silk Road, and its institutions were to be found all the way from the ports of western India to China. Buddhist monuments served as its landmarks, and Buddhist monasteries hosted most travelers. Before the Islamic conquest of portions of India and Central Asia in the eighth century, Buddhist institutions provided the infrastructure all along the eastern Eurasian section of the Silk Road.

In addition to its Buddhist infrastructure, the vitality of the Silk Road continued to depend on the trade of silk, the most prestigious and the most frequently traded commodity. Political changes never stifled the demand for silks; they only affected the structure of the demand and the way the silk markets were supplied.

The Roman Empire's fourth-century transition into the newly formed Byzantine Empire not only shifted the center of the Roman world from Italy to the Balkans and Asia Minor but also made the empire a greater consumer and producer of silk textiles. The Byzantine emperors shed Rome's republican traditions and made their own society more hierarchical. Whereas luxury goods were available to anyone who could afford them in republican times, the Byzantine emperors limited their availability so as to endorse their rule and enhance their different status.

Alongside the elevation of silk, Christianity also rose in the eyes of the Byzantine emperors, who made Constantinople a sacred city of Christianity and the Byzantine Empire a leader of Christendom. The rulers of the empire did not just tolerate the Christians but established their own claims to political legitimacy by lavishing their patronage on the church. According to the Byzantines, the mother of the emperor Constantine had carried the true cross of Jesus Christ to Constantinople, establishing a tradition of the sacred relics of Jesus Christ in the new capital. The Byzantines also claimed that they had obtained the swaddling clothes of Jesus, complete with stains left by the Virgin Mary's milk. In an effort to establish his leadership over the Christian church, Justinian I ordered the construction of an architectural masterpiece, the cathedral Hagia Sophia, or St. Sophia, built between 532 and 537.

With all the gifts Justinian bestowed on the Christian church, the emperor maintained a firm hand over it in Byzantine territories and sought, by military means, the leadership of the entire Christian world. In order to display his vision, Justinian had a symbolic mosaic prepared in the vestibule of Hagia Sophia. In the center of this mosaic, under an arch, the Virgin Mary, patron saint of Constantinople, is sitting on a throne with the baby Jesus on her lap. Constantine the Great, the fourth-century founder of the Byzantine capital, stands on her left, offering Mary a model of the city of Constantinople. Justinian, on her right, is offering the cathedral of Hagia Sophia. Mary is covered with dark purple silk from head to toe, and the two emperors' purple robes are embellished with patterned stripes. All four figures have halos. By situating this mosaic at the doorway of the cathedral, the emperor made his message clear: Mary was the patron of the city and the empire, and the emperors, not the church hierarchy, were her earthly deputies. The entirely purple attire on Mary is the symbol of the most sacred figure, and the silk robes of the emperors, with somewhat less purple, represent a lower status than Mary, but above all other mortals.

Soon after Justinian's general, Belisarius, conquered Italy, the emperor had the cathedral of San Vitale built in Ravenna, on the eastern coast of Italy. Two major mosaics in this church further demonstrate Justinian's wider political intentions. On one of the mosaics, the central figure is the emperor himself, holding the Communion bread and flanked by courtiers, soldiers and priests. His wife, the empress Theodora, is the central figure of another mosaic. Surrounded by male and female courtiers, she is holding a krater of Communion wine. Both the emperor and the empress have halos. As in the mosaic at Hagia Sophia, the clothes of the figures at the center are mainly deep purple. On the pieces at Ravenna, both the emperor and the empress wear robes that are almost entirely purple. His are brocaded with golden thread, while images of the three magi are woven in gold thread on the lower hem of the empress's robe. The courtiers and priests on the two sides of the two major figures all wear some purple, but it fades out in proportion to their distance from the central figures. The designs of these sacred mosaics tell us that purple silk textiles symbolized the greatest power and the highest prestige in the Byzantine Empire. Such imperial uses of silk were a significant factor in the development of a silk industry within the empire and of the maintenance of the Byzantine market position in the international silk trade.

The Byzantine Empire was a much smaller and weaker state than the Roman Empire; but the Byzantines were even richer than the Romans. Silk textiles and purple dye were essential to the regime. The Byzantines inherited these resources from the Roman Empire and then exploited them for political ends. During Roman times, both the purple dye and the silks were expensive but readily available commodities. The Byzantines used these resources to develop a sophisticated silk industry under state monopoly that produced fancy silk textiles comparable in quality to those from China and Sassanid Persia. At this time they were unique in their imperial use of the purple color.[9] In this militarily weak but materially rich state, the silk textiles were used to build and strengthen royal and ecclesiastical hierarchies and were a very useful tool in diplomacy. For instance, after the Bulgarian khan Tervel helped Justinian II to regain his throne in 705, he sent silk cloth and purple leather, along with a license to trade controlled Byzantine goods, to the khan to show his gratitude.[10]

Using silk yarn from China, a silk weaving industry had first appeared in this region in the Phoenician cities of Beirut and Tyre during the Roman period. Although no Roman silk textiles of that age have survived, the author of the *Periplus* includes silk yarn, originally from China, in his list of goods bought from India for sale within the Roman Empire. Tyre was also famous for its purple dye, which was extracted from a shellfish harvested near the eastern coast of the Mediterranean. A large quantity of shellfish produced only a small quantity of dye stuff, making it very costly. Since it was a protein product, the dye suited protein fabrics such as wool so well that it never faded. Tyrean artisans noticed that the purple dye also worked well on silk—also a protein fiber. The combination of silk and purple made the textile very expensive and prestigious. Even so, the Roman ruling elite never restricted the trade or the consumption of purple silks.

Heavily textured silk textiles most attracted the Byzantine emperors. For ritual occasions, emperors and empresses robed themselves in textiles made by compound weaving and dyed in purple or patterned with golden threads. They soon projected the same style onto the Virgin Mary and Jesus Christ. Justinian's government eventually took over the silk weaving industry, mainly in order to establish royal and ecclesiastical hierarchies. The vestments of the royal court and the church showed a strong political sensitivity to the color purple: the darker the purple of the robe, the higher the status of the person wearing it. For those of somewhat lower status in the hierarchies, even the lighter purple or velvet garments were still very desirable.

Justinian made purple silk a government monopoly. As in Roman times, Byzantines in the sixth century had to import all their silk yarn from China, and it still came either by Persian land routes or Indian sea routes. When the supply of yarn was no longer sufficient, Roman artisans unraveled plain silk cloth from China to thread their looms.[11] The filaments were not smooth or long enough to make thin crepe, but they sufficed for the heavier weaves. However, the supply of raw materials for the silk industry remained a serious issue for several centuries. Justinian took advantage of the shortage of silk materials to establish his monopoly. He fixed the price of silk materials at a level lower than the purchasing price from Persia. With no money to be made, private silk dealers gave up the business in Byzantium. Justinian and his successors then purchased all the silk materials coming from foreign countries, thereby monopolizing the supply of silk and securing it for government workshops. Justinian adopted a more aggressive policy for silk materials coming by sea. He made an alliance with Ethiopia to attack the Jewish Himyarite kingdom in Yemen, which controlled access to the Red Sea, and thereby tried to secure the direct shipment of silk materials from India to Byzantine-controlled Egypt.

He even started to introduce sericulture, the process of making silk yarn, in his empire. All these efforts greatly aided the government's monopolization of the silk weaving industry in Byzantium. However, at the end of Justinian's reign, the shortage of silk yarn was still an unsolved problem. A secure supply of domestic silk yarn was only achieved long after his time. Sericulture did eventually develop in other parts of Eurasia besides China, but not until after the Islamic conquests. Nevertheless, Justinian probably did manage to start the process of building a sericulture industry in his homeland, and his successors eventually developed it into a significant industry. He built a silk culture that was an important symbol of the Byzantine court and the hierarchical Christian church. After his time, when the Byzantine state had lost much of its military strength, later Byzantine rulers used the silk textiles and the aura created around them as effective diplomatic weapons with which to protect the imperial interests. The Byzantines often negotiated marriage alliances with German and Islamic rulers, with many silk garments as dowries. In 1100, the Byzantine emperor Alexis I Comnenus presented one hundred purple garments to a German chief.[12]

While other countries in Eurasia also developed silk weaving, China remained the main supplier of both silk yarn and silk textiles, long after the collapse of the Han Empire in the early third century. The political chaos that followed in China actually encouraged the silk trade. The political dynamic between the nomads and the sedentary society continued to promote silk transactions between the steppe and agricultural China; all that changed was that new players were entering the game. Buddhist theology and institutions also were providing a stimulus to the trade. Buddhism and political chaos jointly produced new conditions that encouraged the silk industry and silk culture in China.

In the chaos of civil wars and the rise and fall of ephemeral regimes in the third century, political alliances often crossed the Great Wall. Nomads to the north of the Great Wall were involved in the politics of northern China and were invited to fight alongside one Chinese warlord and against another. During this period, many people on the steppe migrated south of the Great Wall to settle in agricultural lands. Ethnic tensions and oppression by Chinese overlords drove some of these former nomads into rebellion. The successful rebels of nomadic origins thus established many small and short-lived regimes. Ancient Chinese historians called the period encompassing most of the fourth century and the early fifth century "Sixteen States Built by Five Barbarians."

The nearly four centuries between the end of the Han Empire and the beginning of the Sui Empire were a time of significant demographic and social change. Nomads from outside the Great Wall migrated inside, settled there, and were transformed by Chinese culture, and in turn changed Chinese culture as well. Meanwhile, their migrations pushed the northern Chinese population into the marshlands of the south and introduced Chinese culture, including sericulture, to lands in the far south. This process enlarged the territory of Chinese culture. In all of those transitions, silk culture always had a central importance.

Once a nomadic group settled in China as conquerors, they assumed the role of Chinese rulers by sending gifts to the nomads still living on the steppe. The Xianbei were a new power in the north and became the most important player in Chinese politics in the following two centuries. The Tuoba clan of the Xianbei eventually conquered other petty states of nomadic origin in the early fifth century to reinvent themselves as the Northern Wei Dynasty, confronting the Southern Dynasties, of Han descent, in the south.

Soon after the emperor Taiwu, a former nomad, had unified northern China and proclaimed himself founding emperor of the Northern Wei, a chief of the Tuyuhun, nomads from the region of modern Qinghai Province, sent an envoy to his court. The nomadic chief expressed his goodwill and his desire to maintain friendly relations with the Northern Wei ruler and help him defend the border against other nomads. Meanwhile, he demanded gifts, mostly silk regalia, from the Northern Wei court. He argued that his regime had adopted the Chinese way of using chariots and displaying standards, but the gifts he received from China were not sufficient to maintain this level of civilization. The inexperienced emperor presented the case to his courtiers for discussion. They consulted the archives of the Han court and after some deliberation, advised the emperor to modestly increase the quantity, based on the Tuyuhuns' contributions to the defense of the border and their status among other steppe nomads.[13] Giving silk gifts to chiefs on the steppe would verify Taiwu's status as a Chinese emperor in the eyes of the nomads. Diplomacy with the nomads was mandatory for a Chinese ruler. Since the dynamics of the relationship between the powers in agricultural China and those on the steppe continued, Chinese silk continued to flow to the steppe as before.

After Emperor Taiwu, the Northern Wei rulers adopted more Han Chinese ways as means of bolstering their legitimacy. Their steppe religion would not be suitable for the ruler of an agricultural society, but Confucianism, the official ideology of the Han Empire, did not suit either. In the post-Han chaos, most educated Chinese still followed Confucian doctrines such as filial piety. However, the cornerstone of Confucianism, a paternal monarchy based on a patriarchal family system, was not practical in a time of migrations. After the nomads entered north China, many Chinese fled to the south. Many people lost their family ties and could no longer remember the lineages of their ancestors.

Meanwhile, Buddhism, the new religion, provided new community centers. People desperately looking for a safety net in the form of communities regrouped around Buddhist monasteries. Adopting Confucianism as the state religion was not acceptable to many nobles of the Northern Wei royal lineage, who took pride in their steppe traditions, nor was it appealing to their Chinese subjects. Buddhism was the obvious choice. From 460 on, the Northern Wei emperor began to have huge statues of the Buddha carved near the capital, Pingcheng (present-day Yungang), in the northern part of present Shanxi Province. Those statues, monuments marking the eastern end of the Silk Road, represented the reincarnations of the current and former rulers of the Northern Wei. Through these carvings, the Northern Wei emperors declared themselves the representatives of the Buddha and therefore the legitimate rulers of China.

In 471, Emperor Xiaowen ascended the throne and further reformed the Northern Wei regime. He changed his Tuoba surname—and also the name of the clan—to a Chinese surname, Yuan, meaning "original." He also made eight noble Tuoba clans change their family names to Chinese surnames. These families formed the aristocracy, or ruling elite, of the regime, and they remained distinguished lineages in China alongside the indigenous Chinese aristocracy. Another major step was to move the capital from Pingcheng, on the border between the agricultural area and the land of nomads, to Luoyang, in the Yellow River Valley, the core of ancient Chinese civilization. To legitimize this action, Xiaowen ordered new statues of the Buddha carved at a site, Longmen, near the new capital and had a new state monastery built with the same name and form as the one in the previous capital.

The huge statues provided the most spectacular symbol of the Northern Wei state's patronage of Buddhism. From that time, the new Buddhist grottoes at Longmen became the site where both rulers and commoners demonstrated their faith in Buddhism. They donated money to have caves excavated along the cliff, and to have statues of Buddhas and bodhisattvas carved in the caves. Longmen became the largest center of Buddhist art in Central China in the Northern Dynasties period, and continued to be so into the Sui and Tang dynasties.

The patronage of Buddhism was deeply entwined with the promotion of silk production, an important duty of a Chinese ruler. The Northern Wei court was the first Chinese regime to distribute abandoned land to peasants to encourage the cultivation of food crops and of mulberry trees for silks. Plain silk textiles were a major part of the tax that farming households paid to the government, so silk production picked up quickly. Following the model of the Han Empire, the Northern Wei rulers also enacted sumptuary laws, declaring that only the ruling elite was entitled to wear fine silk textiles, namely brocades and embroidered cloth. To enforce this law, the government had all silk weaving artisans registered, and all the exquisite silk textiles were woven in state-run workshops. Anyone, be he a prince or a trader, who ran private workshops to make certain luxuries, including fine silks, faced the death penalty.[14] The fancy silk textiles produced under government control were used to make the ritual clothes for the court and special robes for foreign rulers, including those from the steppe, and for the Buddhist monasteries. The maintenance of the prestige and aura of exquisite silk textiles through restrictions placed on the market and on consumption was yet another means for rulers of nomadic origins to provide themselves with a Chinese identity.

By the fifth and sixth centuries, Buddhism in China was no longer a religion solely for rulers and foreigners. When the Northern Wei rulers had large caves excavated and huge statues of the Buddha carved, people of lesser status followed their example and had smaller statues sculpted. Those who could not afford the small statues on their own pooled their resources to make donations to the monasteries so as to have statues of the Buddha and various bodhisattvas built under their collective names. Three to four centuries after Buddhist institutions and artworks in Bactria and Gandhara helped the nomadic Yuezhi transform themselves into the Kushans, with their King of Kings ruling over an agricultural empire, Buddhist monasteries and statues similarly helped transform the Tuoba chiefs into the emperors of the Northern Wei Dynasty.

While Buddhist monuments changed the landscape of China, Mahayana Buddhist concepts of the cosmos and cycles of life took root in the minds of the Chinese people. People believed that donations made to the Buddha and bodhisattvas via the monasteries that housed their images could ensure a better future life or might even save a life in this world. This belief channeled great wealth into Buddhist monasteries, whose numbers increased rapidly. Luoyang alone had more than 1,000 monasteries.[15]

Buddhist monasteries soon became the largest consumers of luxury goods in the empires. Ruling elites, rich merchants, and even poor commoners made donations according to the instructions of Mahayana Buddhist texts. A group of Mahayana Buddhist texts composed under the Kushan Empire, including the *Lotus Sutra* and the *Western Pure Land Sutra,* were translated into readable Chinese. These scriptures encouraged devotees to make donations of luxuries that were a part of Silk Road trade. Contemporary literature and modern archaeological surveys show that the people of the Northern Wei, the upper and lower social strata, followed these instructions literally and gave the Seven Treasures, as well as silk textiles, to Buddhist monasteries as donations and decorations for statues and stupas. In the ruins of the Yongning Stupa, the official state stupa of the Northern Wei at Luoyang, archaeologists found pieces of gem beads during an excavation in the 1980s, some 1,400 years after the complex burned down.[16]

Despite restrictions on using and trading certain luxury goods, nothing could stop devotees from purchasing fancy silk textiles and imported gems and incense as donations to the monasteries. The rulers who imposed the restrictions were conscious of the consequences of stopping this religious devotion, as they themselves had accepted the Buddhist idea of retribution. Had they tried to stop the trading and donation of the luxuries to the monasteries, they would have had to face dire consequences in their own future lives. The Northern Wei and the northern governments that succeeded them did not vigorously enforce the code. The merchants who had the means to buy the luxuries were the most likely to ignore these sumptuary laws and purchase costly goods for devotions. In the end, the emperors' own patronage of Buddhism encouraged commoners to breach the sumptuary laws and eventually made the restrictions almost obsolete.

Consequently, at the time of the Northern Dynasties, many imported goods flowed into northern China. Archaeologists have found many foreign-made goods in the tombs of wealthy people of this period. Among the finery found in the tomb of Li Xian, an early sixth-century general and statesman, was a gilded silver ewer. This ewer belongs to a group of similarly gilded silver vases made in Tukharistan, the land of Bactria and the Kushans in Afghanistan. The postures of the six human figures are typical of the Bactrian-Hellenistic period, but the ewer was made long after the demise of Greek Bactria and the Kushans' regime.

Foreign-made silk textiles were among the many exotic items imported into China. Quite a few have survived in graves in the Turfan region on the Central Asian Silk Road. Some fragments found in this arid region show definite non-Chinese styles and weaving methods. In the same graves where these silks have been found, archaeologists have uncovered documents referring to silk brocades made in Persia, India, and Byzantium. By the fifth and sixth centuries, China was no longer the sole producer of silk textiles. Chinese consumers welcomed foreign silks because they found the exotic artistic styles attractive, and because these fancy textiles, just as sophisticated as the Chinese ones, were not under government monopoly.

Persian silk pieces were wider than the Chinese ones, and the sophisticated patterns on them were larger than those the Chinese produced. It is no wonder that Iranian silk textiles became a hot commodity in China, the homeland of the silk industry. Sassanid Persia became the Byzantine government's partner in the Eurasian trade. The Persians sold to the Byzantines what they obtained from China, either directly, or indirectly through the Sogdians. Meanwhile, the Persians established their own silk weaving industry, which produced high-quality, fancy textiles. Since the time when the Achaemenids ruled Persia, the Iranian monarchy had surrounded itself with luxury. Woolen tapestries and rugs had long been Iran's most famous products and were much sought after by the Han Empire. By applying the weaving technology of woolen textiles to shiny silk yarn, Iranian artisans produced a unique style of textile.

So far, no silk textiles made during Sassanid rule have been found within the boundaries of Iran. Scholars have listed many silk samples found outside the empire's boundaries as "Sassanid" because their decorative features bear a strong resemblance to the motifs on the robes of the Sassanid kings whose full-bodied images were carved in bas-relief on rock faces. The simurgh, a common royal motif on Sassanid silver vases and other artistic media, is displayed on the robe of the Sassanid king Khusro II, on the statue of him riding his horse, among the government-sponsored rock carvings at Tak-i-Bustan. The simurgh must have been a pattern used on royal silk textiles. In addition, several pieces of silk textiles dated to the Sassanid period have been found in European Christian churches and Central Asian tombs, and they include simurghs in their designs. It is now generally accepted that the simurgh motif originated in Sassanid Iran.

Other notable designs probably of the same origin are two horses in some sort of confrontation and hunting scenes. The equestrian motif represented the divinity of Sassanid kingship. The rock relief of the founder of the Sassanid Dynasty, Ardashir I, receiving investiture from Ahura Mazda portrays both the Zoroastrian god and the king riding on horses. The scene of two horseback riders confronting each other inspired numerous artworks in Iran and other Eurasian countries later influenced by Iran.

Persian silk weavers learned from earlier Roman artisans. When the Sassanid army occupied the Mediterranean coast, they took Roman Empire artisans as prisoners and relocated them in Iran to work for them.[17] Control over this coastal region later shifted between the Byzantines and the Persians. Weavers who were oppressed or deprived of their livelihoods under Justinian fled to the Sassanid domain to make a living.[18] Sassanid Persia and Byzantium not only competed for silk materials but also became rivals in the production of prestigious textiles, as they soon possessed the same technical skills, given the frequent movement of the artisans. Even though the Byzantines held the Persians in contempt, Sassanid motifs, such as the simurgh and the equestrian themes, were commonly found on Byzantine silk textiles in the centuries after Justinian.

Until the end of the Sassanid Dynasty, the rivalry between the Byzantines and Persians seriously hindered the supply of raw materials for the looms of Constantinople. China still held its position as the major producer of silk yarn, especially the highest quality yarn with long filaments, and steppe nomads continued to carry Chinese silks westward. To circumvent Persian-controlled land routes directly to their east, the Byzantines looked north for access to steppe routes. In the early sixth century, a new nomadic power, the Turks, appeared on the northern border of China. They frequented the Great Wall gates to purchase silks and silk floss, and they soon became major players in the exchange of silk and horses outside the Great Wall. The Turks, like their predecessors on the steppe, not only controlled the steppe routes to the west but also had a good relationship with specialized commercial communities who had much experience on the Silk Road, especially the Sogdians. The Turks, the dominant force on the steppe after the sixth century, obtained a great deal of silk yarn from China and also had access to the steppe routes. In turn, the Sogdian traders, who by this time were active throughout Eurasia, saw great profit in selling silks for the Turks.

According to the Byzantine historian Menander the Protector, in the latter part of the sixth century a group of Sogdian traders, representing the Turks, went to see the Sassanid king, Khusro, and asked for permission to sell Chinese silks in Persia. Khusro feared that Chinese silks might take a significant amount of the market away from locally made silks. He offered to buy the silks at a good price and then burned them in front of the delegation, implying that these silks were worth nothing in Persia.

The humiliated Sogdians returned home very unhappy, but they still wanted to find a market for the silks that the Turks had in their possession. A Sogdian chief merchant, Maniakh, persuaded the chief of the Turks to take their silks to the Byzantines, since the Byzantines used more silks than all other peoples. The Turkish chief, Sizabu, commissioned Maniakh as the Turks' ambassador to Byzantium. Around the year 571, the Byzantine emperor Justin II received the delegation and sent a mission out to the Turks to negotiate the trade.[19] This is only one instance of Sogdian traders operating as commercial middlemen between nomadic and sedentary states.

As traders, the Sogdians had gained extensive knowledge about silks and their production, and at some point they began weaving silks in their own homeland. By the late sixth century, they were producing one of the most popular silks in Eurasia, a silk known at the time as Zandaniji. Its name came from Zandan, a village near the city of Bukhara. Its patterns resembled those of the Sassanids, in that they often featured stiff animal motifs such as birds and rams. However, the colors, and probably the silk yarn as well, were Chinese. Whereas

Zandanijian silk brocade, produced in the town called Zandan, near Bukhara, became a famous textile all over Eurasia with its paired, majestic but stiff animal motifs. Many similar samples have been found in church treasuries in Europe and at Buddhist sites in Central Asia. © Victoria and Albert Museum, London

Persian silks were often woven in somber colors such as dark blue and gray, the Zandaniji silks often combined chartreuse, orange, and pink to create their patterns—a very Chinese color scheme. The production of Zandaniji silks continued even after the Islamic conquests in Central Asia. More than a hundred sample pieces of Zandaniji silks have been identified.[20] Most of them were preserved in religious institutions, such as churches in Europe and Buddhist caves in Dunhuang, which was on the Central Asian Silk Road. In recent years, some Zandaniji silks have been found outside the religious institutions, in various graves along the Silk Road. In a burial site of local chiefs at a place called Moshchevaja Balka, on a route through the Caucasus region (between the Black Sea and the Caspian Sea), scholars have found many pieces of silk textiles, some Zandaniji, from all over Eurasia.[21] Many pieces of well-preserved Zandaniji silk have been found recently in the tombs of early Tibetan chiefs in Dulan (in modern Qinghai Province). The

Sogdians must have not only carried the silks of other countries but also sold silk products made in their own homeland.

In the fourth century, the Sassanid governors of Iran, overwhelmed by new waves of nomads, namely the Hephthalites and the Turks, gradually lost control of what had been the northern part of the Kushan territories. At about the same time, an indigenous Indian regime, the Gupta Dynasty, rose in the middle and Lower Ganges Plain. Unlike that of the Kushan Empire, the Gupta economy was based more on agriculture than on trade. The Guptas' power extended across much of the northern Indian plain, including the Mathura region, but barely reached to the subcontinent's northwestern region. Even though the Guptas sought to distinguish themselves from the Kushans, a regime of foreign origin, by endorsing orthodox Brahmanical traditions, the Gupta rulers inherited many customs from the Kushans. The Gupta kings also minted gold coins, and the images of kings on those coins were depicted in robes similar in style to those of the Kushans, or in the style of horse-riding peoples. More important, the new rulers inherited a taste for rare commodities from abroad, and thereby sustained the market for the luxurious goods the Silk Road trade provided.

Literature, art, and architecture all represented the refined lifestyle of the Gupta elite, and among the fineries they most enjoyed were the silk textiles from China. The Gupta Empire, like other sedentary states, had also established its own silk weaving industry. India had its own indigenous species of silkworm, but it differed from those the Chinese used. Because the Indian worm produced a different sort of silk and Indian artisans had not mastered the technique of making long filaments out of silk cocoons, Chinese silk textiles remained the most coveted. From the works of that era's prolific poets, it is apparent that silk textiles were necessary not only for ritual occasions but also for enhancing the beauty of the ladies. Refined and elaborate, the stone sculptures of the Gupta period—including those of the Buddha—were carved to show a layer of clothing so fine as to expose the contours of the body. In addition to the secular market, religious establishments, especially Buddhist monasteries, became large-scale consumers of imported silk textiles. The Seven Treasures remained the preferred gifts for the Buddha and bodhisattvas, but silk banners and festoons decorated many stupas and statues, as prescribed by Mahayana Buddhist texts.

Thanks to the Buddhist establishments built up during the Kushan period, the trade routes through the northwest—either the area formerly known as Bactria or the Upper Indus Valley—were still viable, despite the decline or total disappearance of the many urban centers that had flourished during Kushan times. Buddhist stupas along the trade routes developed into pilgrimage sites, attracting both devotees and traders. The monasteries that enclosed the stupas provided both facilities and guidance for the travelers on the trade routes. The routes crossing both the Hindu Kush and the Upper Indus Valley were dangerous and difficult. Pilgrims and traders both often called on their religious faith for courage. Most of the traders were Buddhists.

The nomads who were new to the region did not disturb but, in fact, encouraged the trade. The Hephthalites, or the White Huns, minted silver coins according to Kushan standards, though the quality was much lower due to their lack of experience in commerce. Given the very basic facilities, it was brave traders such as the Sogdians, whose faith was Buddhism, who traveled to India. Buddhist pilgrims from China also reached India in the early fifth century. One Buddhist teacher, Faxian, started his travels, accompanied by several monks, in 399 and returned to China in 416. He crossed the Pamir Plateau and proceeded to the Indus Valley. He visited many sacred Buddhist sites in the northwest before descending to the Ganges plain, the birthplace of Buddhism. All along the route, he noticed silk banners hanging on stupas and carried in festival parades, and that these textiles were essential for the Buddhist liturgy in India. Many groups of Chinese pilgrims followed in the footsteps of Faxian. About a century after his journey, the Northern Wei ruler, an empress dowager, sent a group of pilgrims representing her court to Gandhara. They came with a whole caravan of silk products. In the mid-sixth century, Yang Xuanzhi, a scholar who criticized the Buddhist extravagance of his time, reported: "when they started from the capital city, the empress dowager granted 1,000 banners of five-colored silk about 30 meters in length, and 500 incense bags made of silk brocade. Princes and ministers also donated 2,000 silk banners."[22]

Pilgrims facilitated the trade. Even though they donated these goods to monasteries, the monasteries could turn them back into commodities by selling them. Buddhist establishments along this section of the Silk Road actually sustained the long-distance trade in luxuries during an age of weakened governments and insecurity.

The continuing trade along the Silk Road, in spite of constant political turmoil both on the steppe and in agricultural regions, meant that the Silk Road had matured. It had gained a physical presence and infrastructure, with numerous large and small landmarks, and a deeply religious yet pluralist culture embracing travelers from all backgrounds and directions. Its vitality depended no longer on the sponsorship of one or several imperial powers but now on market forces—the supply and demand for trade goods in countries all across Eurasia.

CHAPTER 5

Transforming the Eurasian Silk Market

Describing the feelings and attitude of a soldier serving on the Chinese empire's western frontier during the Tang Dynasty, the eighth-century poet Wang Han wrote:

> Holding a glowing goblet filled with grape wine,
> Following the melody of a lute, I am about to drink,
> The neighing horse urges me to ride him.
> Do not laugh if you see me lying drunk on the battlefield,
> Few soldiers ever come back from western expeditions anyway.[1]

In the seventh century, some four hundred years after the Han Empire had retreated from the Western Region, the Tang Empire garrisoned the western section of the Great Wall and established its suzerainty over the Tarim Basin and the oasis towns that dot the edges of its Takla Makan Desert. Imperial protection and patronage of the Silk Road stimulated the long-distance trade in luxuries to even greater heights. Camel caravans carrying exotic commodities arrived in droves at the gates of the Great Wall. No longer was it only the ruling elite who could enjoy the imported grape wine in glass goblets and the fine music played on a lute, an instrument that originated in India. Even soldiers and commoners could enjoy the grape wine. It was, of course, the soldiers, most of whom were drafted from the population of taxpaying farmers, who paid with their youth or even their lives the price for the booming foreign trade and urban prosperity. The soldier's sentiment regarding his frontier life became one of the predominant themes of Tang literature.

To bring imperial glory to the Western Region, the Tang founders first had to build a centralized, strong state. When the Li family took power in China and founded the Tang Dynasty, they faced the opposition of many influential aristocratic families that had flourished during the centuries of political division. The Tang rulers intended to deprive these families of their local or regional political power and then to build an empire with a strong central government and a centrally appointed bureaucracy that would reach all the way down to the local county level. Nobles from the nomadic tribes and aristocratic Chinese literati fiercely resisted this plan, attempting to protect their political and social privileges. The seventh century, the first century of Tang rule, was filled with bloody struggles between the new imperial power and the aristocracies. In these power struggles, silk robes of various colors, which were worn in court rituals, would play an essential role in establishing the power of the imperial bureaucracy.

To help unify China under one government, the Tang rulers replaced the traditional hereditary government service system with a Confucian meritocracy. Under the new system, passing particular levels of government examinations entitled scholars to specific official positions. During the Tang Empire, a substantial number of government officials, but not all, were recruited through this channel. The candidates who passed were given rank in the bureaucracy according to their rank in the examinations. Thereafter, promotion or demotion was performance based. To bring prestige to the men who succeeded in the examination system, the seventh-century empress Wu Zetian created a new list of important families as a counter to the aristocracy. Whoever was above the fifth rank in this nine-rank system joined the circle of the new "aristocracy," which was a hierarchy whose members' ranks were subject to change based on their performance.

Tang rulers designated special colors and designs for the official robes of each rank. Tang emperors and ministers wore trousers and boots with knee-length robes that had slits on both sides, an equestrian outfit suitable for hunting or playing polo, both fashionable pastimes of the elite. Purple remained the most prestigious color throughout the period. Yellow, the traditional color of the emperor, was still designated exclusively for his ritual robes, but even emperors wore purple robes for daily business.[2] All candidates taking the imperial examination dreamed of the day that they could wear purple robes.

The prestige attached to the color purple was a clear deviation from orthodox Confucian values. Confucius had considered red the purest and most virtuous color and had condemned purple for its impurity, since it was not a primary color, and for its pretension to redness. By Tang times, the hierarchy of symbolic colors used by rulers had changed, most likely due to the influence of foreign rulers' preferences. After seeing the Byzantine silk textiles and hearing of the fabled color purple, the Chinese also dyed their silks this color, although the dye stuff they used was botanical, unlike the costly Tyrian dye extracted from eastern Mediterranean shellfish.

The Tang government had all the exquisite textiles intended for official robes made in state-run workshops. To set up a private shop that imitated imperial styles was to risk one's head. The purple robe in Tang China indicated elevated status, but it was the status of merit in addition to birth. An early Tang era book entitled *Anecdotes Inside and Outside the Tang Court* tells the story of the lifelong friendship of the founding emperor, Taizong, and Wang Xian, his childhood friend. The two boys often played together and joked with each other. The future emperor teased Wang Xian, saying that he would not be able to make a cocoon for himself, like a silkworm, until he had reached old age, implying that he would have no achievement until late in life. After the emperor was on the throne, his childhood friend came to ask a favor: "Can I make a cocoon now?" The emperor smiled and said he was not sure yet. The emperor then granted positions to the sons of Wang Xian, but not Wang Xian himself, because he was not qualified. Wang petitioned again, saying that he was willing to die the night of the day he received the honor. The emperor granted him a position that entitled him to wear the purple robe and golden belt, and, true to his word, Wang Xian died that night.[3] The moral of the story was that a purple robe for those who did not deserve it was a curse.

But even the most rigorous sumptuary laws could not prevent the wearing of purple robes by those who aspired to high style and had the means of doing so and the nerve to take the risk. Although the Tang court reissued the restrictions on purple silk and other high-quality silks repeatedly, there were continued reports of offenses. Rich merchants hid their offense, secretly enjoying the textile's prestige by lining their robes with it. If merchants and other well-to-do people could not obtain government-produced silks, they went to other sources. Products from Persia, India, Central Asia, and the Byzantine Empire had long found their way to the Chinese market and were readily available. Foreign silk textiles became profitable for Chinese merchants. Yangzhou on the Lower Yangzi River became a center for the reproduction and sale of these products. They were very luxurious silks that anyone could buy because they did not carry the imperial designs that indicated exclusive government use.

Another major breach of the sumptuary laws had its origin in the government's relationship with various religious institutions. Tang rulers granted purple robes to the most respected priests of several different faiths. Unlike the Byzantine Empire, Tang China had no single dominant state religion. The Buddhists were the most populous religious group, and outstanding monks received many purple robes as well as other sorts of robes made of exquisite silk textiles. Nestorian Christians, who arrived in China in the late seventh century, also received the honor of the purple robes from the Tang court.

When the Buddhist priest Xuanzang reached old age, he petitioned the emperor for funds to build a stupa for storing the precious Buddhist texts he had brought back from India. The emperor did not give him cash but granted him a great deal of silk clothing from deceased women in his harem.[4] These beautiful silk clothes were forbidden commodities under normal conditions, yet they could not be reused in the royal palaces, since the demise of those who had once worn them made them impure. Buddhist monasteries, in the business of funerals and securing the afterlife, could well receive those donations and convert them into needed funds by selling them in the marketplace.

These Buddhist religious activities, while creating a substantial breach in the government's monopoly on exquisite silk textiles, nevertheless sustained the trade on the Silk Road and facilitated international commerce by adding to the infrastructure that had been growing ever since Kushan times. When Buddhist monks traveled to India on pilgrimages, they carried silk textiles, which could be used as cash. The silks often came to them in the form of religious donations, and they were obliged to bless the donors. In exchange for lodgings and other facilities, the pilgrims gave the silks to monasteries along the routes as religious donations. When Xuanzang set off for India from China in 630, the Tang government refused him travel documents because they were at war with the Turks. Undeterred, he approached the ruler of Gaochang, in the oasis of Turfan, just outside the Tang frontier of that time. From this ruler, he received thirty horse-loads of treasures, mostly silk textiles, as his travel funds. Following his example, Chinese pilgrims in the Tang period all solicited quantities of silk in China before traveling by land or by sea. After establishing contacts in India and returning home, some pilgrims also sent gifts of silk textiles to their acquaintances in India, which they asked traders to deliver for them. Teachers and preachers of Buddhism in India also continued to travel to China. There they received many silks as rewards for their religious services from the emperors and other members of the royal court and from patrons among the commoners.[5] Traders, whether Indian, Sogdian, or Chinese, often accompanied pilgrims and preachers. They shared the same facilities and donated to monasteries along the Silk Road in the same manner. They probably carried many silks and other products, though this is not as well documented.

At the western end of the Silk Road, religious activities also sustained the silk trade. Since the time of Justinian, Byzantine emperors had contrived to hold leadership of all Christendom. Their major competitors were the popes in Rome. Rome had a number of advantages over the Byzantines in terms of religious prestige. It had once been the diocese of Saint Peter, who held the key to heaven's gate, according to Christian tradition. Moreover, Rome was the place where many saints had been martyred in the early days of Christianity, and pilgrims were attracted by their relics. The Byzantines, on the other hand, controlled all the materials needed to make a cathedral look like paradise. With improved technology, Byzantine looms produced textiles of more and more sophisticated designs. Many textiles depicted Christian themes, such as the Annunciation and the Nativity. Weaving the figures of the Virgin Mary, Jesus Christ, and the saints demanded highly sophisticated techniques and extraordinary artistic skills. In all the sacred figural designs, Mary and Jesus invariably wore purple silk robes.

The continuing development of Byzantine silk textiles made them extremely precious. Byzantine rulers, with deliberate calculation, released limited amounts of silk with royal and Christian themes to Rome and to churches in western Europe. All the churches that sprang up in Europe after the fifth and sixth centuries required relics of saints to embellish their altars and exquisite silk textiles to cover them. While pilgrims and thieves thronged to Rome for the sacred relics, silk textiles had to come from Byzantine territory. In addition to Bibles, priests dispatched by the Roman church to other parts of Europe required at least one set of vestments made of Byzantine silks.

All Christians, rich or poor, common or noble, wanted to be buried near holy relics. Kings were surely privileged in this regard, and after Charlemagne, their bodies were also wrapped in Byzantine silks with royal designs. Byzantine silks became the symbol of royalty as well as sanctity. The entire traffic in Byzantine silk textiles to the West might not have been on a large scale, but it still constituted a serious leak in the Byzantine silk monopoly. In the West, Christian religious belief made the acquisition, by legal or illegal means, of precious silks from the Byzantine looms a religiously meritorious achievement. Christian religious activities such as pilgrimage and church construction eventually compromised the Byzantine monopoly—a monopoly even more rigid than that of the Chinese—and their silks continued to flow to the West.

The Byzantine Empire quickly shrank after Justinian's death, but Byzantium was still the most affluent state in the western part of Eurasia.

The court of Byzantium set the fashion for the rising European rulers, and the liturgy of the Byzantine church became the model for the new churches in Europe. Since the Byzantine Empire was the only producer of high-quality silk textiles in the West, silk was still an effective tool for diplomacy in the emperors' efforts to manage domestic and international crises. As already mentioned, Byzantine rulers often used silks to make political allies, sending silk gifts to the powers in the Islamic world as well as the rising powers in western Europe. From the eighth century, they negotiated and arranged more than sixteen marriages with the German empire. Many envoys were dispatched from Constantinople to the West with gifts and dowries.

Byzantine rulers defended their monopoly on silk textiles and purple dye, among their last effective weapons in defending their empire, to the end. In the mid-tenth century, Bishop Liudprand of Cremona visited Byzantium as an envoy of Otto I of Germany. When he was leaving, the border officials confiscated all the purple silks he had purchased, explaining, "As we surpass all other nations in wealth and wisdom, so it is right that we should surpass them in dress."[6] Even his protest in the name of his church did not help him to get back the silks. Another border official ordered Liudprand to come ashore after he had already boarded his ship. The official, whose name was Michael, was so meticulous in his duties that he inspected the interior of the bishop's cloak to see whether there was a purple silk lining hidden underneath the surface.

The Byzantine rulers clung to their purple silk monopoly so firmly that Christians outside the empire never learned the technology of making the purple dye. Sometime around the year 895, the Byzantine emperor, Leo VI, issued an edict to the eparch (mayor) of Constantinople, now known as *The Book of the Eparch*. Among the many ordinances dealing with various affairs of the city, there is a special section devoted to the rules regarding "Merchants of Silk Stuffs." Silk merchants in Constantinople were strictly banned from selling purple dyed silks to the people on the prohibited list, lest they export.

When Constantinople fell to the Turks in 1453, the Byzantine dyeing technique was lost to posterity. As a consequence, the Roman church had to change the color of the vestments of its high officials (cardinals) and other sacerdotal textiles from purple to a scarlet that was achieved by means of a dye made from cochineal insects.[7] New Islamic sources would now supply Christian Europe with silk yarn and textiles in quantity—minus the most craved purple color—and eventually would change the circumstances and the nature of the Eurasian silk market.

From as early as the seventh century, the trading networks built during the time of the Islamic caliphates had been another major threat to the Byzantine monopoly on the western European silk trade. The Islamic conquest of various parts of western Asia and much of northern Africa in the seventh century was rapid and sweeping. Silk shops in the Byzantine Middle East and Sassanid Iran, and, later on in Central Asia, all produced silk textiles for the Islamic regimes. Whereas Byzantine silk was relatively scarce because of the emperors' monopoly and Tang silk, though abundant, was severely restricted by the Chinese government, none of the silk produced under Muslim auspices was forbidden to anyone. By the end of the eighth century, the technology of the production of silk threads from silkworms had spread all the way from Central Asia to the Middle East and North Africa and even to the southern part of Muslim-controlled Spain (though even after silk weaving and sericulture were established in Islamic world, silk remained an expensive textile in the West).

The story of the Islamic silk trade begins with the first Islamic empire, the Umayyad Caliphate (661–750), which was based in Damascus, Syria. The caliphate was overwhelmed by the problems of dealing with the material wealth that came under its control and by questions about the status of converts from conquered lands. Early conquests brought in a tremendous amount of booty. Soon after the initial Islamic conquests, debate arose about who should and should not enjoy the luxuries that came as booty from the conquered peoples. Religious teachers advised the new rulers to be frugal and keep themselves distant from the corrupting effect of luxuries. But political and economic reality did not permit the new rulers to lead such reclusive lives. Facing the religious and administrative challenges of running a large empire, Islamic rulers would build a state-supervised textile industry and market that would exert great influence on the silk trade of Eurasia.

The new lands under Islamic rule were rich countries with ancient civilizations, populated with sophisticated and educated peoples, who produced many desirable products. Although the soldiers of the new Arab empire were largely drawn from nomadic Bedouin tribes, not all Arabs were unfamiliar with the products and cultures of urban centers. Islam arose in the Arabian caravan cities, and Muhammad himself had been a trader who dealt with foreign products, including textiles. New converts, particularly Persians, began to allege that they were far more sophisticated than the Arabs and should therefore assume leadership within Islamic society. The caliphs realized that their conquered peoples, along with their material wealth, possessed a more sumptuous and literate culture than their own. In fact, the Arab elite became immersed in the cultures of the conquered peoples. Talented individuals from Persia were courtiers of their court. Beautiful women captured as slaves from conquered countries filled the harem of the caliph and the households of Arab nobles. Most caliphs married slave women who had come from conquered peoples; these wives naturally exposed their children, including future caliphs, to their own cultures. Since the Islamic religion never forbade the mingling or intermarriage of slaves and masters, the enslaved women of the palace soon became a part of the elite, and their fashions became the fashions of the society at large.

The tension between the right to enjoy material wealth and the duty of the commander of the faithful was so great in the early Islamic regime that when the Umayyad Caliphate was overthrown, its rulers were accused of corruption. The Arab historian Mas'udi (896–956) relates an interesting anecdote about the end of the Umayyad Caliphate in his book *The Meadows of Gold*. When the son of the last Umayyad caliph fled to Nubia for refuge, the Nubian king accused him of enjoying such things as brocades, silk, and gold, which were forbidden by the *Quran*. The young man retorted: "As power fled from us, we called upon the support of alien races who have entered our faith and we have adopted these clothes from them."[8] In fact, the Quran did not forbid silk, gold, or any luxuries. Moreover, in the paradise the Quran describes, people were well supplied with silk as well as gold and pearls. However, the Hadith, the collected sayings of Muhammad, did instruct the Arabs not to wear silk garments, for those who enjoyed the luxuries of this world, it was said, would be deprived of them in the next.[9]

Contrary to this advice, the Abbasid Caliphate (749–1258), which succeeded the Umayyad, established a far more opulent lifestyle. The Abbasids' capital, Baghdad, was a larger, grander city than Damascus. The Abbasids controlled a larger territory and had more government workshops, which produced all manner of goods, so Islamic commercial networks now spread to most parts of Eurasia. The Arab rulers and urban elites now enjoyed every luxury, especially textiles. The Arabs, as well as many of their subjects, had come from tent cultures, in which carpets, rugs, and tapestries were common. After they began to settle in palaces, they decorated the stone or marble walls, floors, and roofs in the same style as their tents.

The Islamic rulers extended this treatment to religious structures as well. The Kaaba, the building at the very center of the Islamic pilgrimage, has been covered by a black silk velvet cloth since the time of the Abbasid Caliphate. So much cloth was quite costly. The silk cover

The Kaaba in Mecca, the cubical structure housing the sacred rock that is the center of worship in the Islamic world, has been covered with black silk velvet since the Abbasid times. The best material, velvet, was used to demonstrate devotion to Islam. Muslim dignitaries vie for the privilege of donating the cover, which needs to be replaced annually. Library of Congress, LC-DIG-matpc-04658 had to be replaced annually to ensure it was in good condition. The names and titles of the donors were inscribed on the edge of the cover and were seen by the pilgrims. The privilege of donating this covering was a claim of legitimacy granted by God, and the caliphs in Baghdad could well afford it during the period when they were powerful and rich. After the caliphate weakened in the tenth century, various local Islamic regimes vied with each other for the privilege of donating the cover of the Kaaba.

To assert their authority as Commanders of the Faithful, the Abbasid caliphs would grant a vassal robes of black satin, each with a golden *tiraz,* or embroidered border; a gold necklace; a pair of gold bracelets; a sword with a gold covered scabbard; a horse with a gold saddle; and a black silk standard with the name of the caliph written on it in white. The caliphs set up factories in Baghdad to produce these official silk robes and standards, as well as colorful robes of honor to reward both generals who won battles and scholars who made cultural contributions.

The Abbasid Caliphate was one of the richest states in the medieval world, and Baghdad was one of the most cosmopolitan cities of the time. All kinds of wealth came to Baghdad. In a collection of stories written during the Abbasid Caliphate known as the *Arabian Nights,* one encounters many exotic commodities with strange names, including textiles from Rum (a common term for Byzantium), China, Persia, Egypt, and Central Asia. When the real-life caliph Harun al-Rashid, the hero of many of the stories in the *Arabian Nights,* died in 809, the treasures he left behind, as recorded by Ibn al-Zubayr (a not-well-known Arab writer), were most impressive:[10]

4,000	embroidered robes
4,000	silk cloaks, lined with sable, mink and other furs
10,000	caftans
2,000	drawers of various kinds
4,000	turbans
1,000	hoods
1,000	capes of various kinds
5,000	kerchiefs of different kinds
500	pieces of velvet
100,000	*mithqals* of musk
100,000	*mithqals* of ambergris
1,000	baskets of India aloes
1,000	precious china (porcelain) vessels

	Many kinds of perfume
	Jewels valued by the jewelers at
	4 million dinars
500,000	dinars (cash)
1,000	jeweled rings
1,000	Armenian carpets
4,000	curtains
5,000	cushions
5,000	pillows
1,500	silk carpets
100	silk rugs
1,000	silk cushions and pillows
300	Maysānī carpets
1,000	Darabjirdi carpets
1,000	cushions with silk brocade
1,000	inscribed silk cushions
1,000	silk curtains
300	silk brocade curtains
500	Ṭabarī carpets
1,000	Ṭabarī cushions
1,000	pillows (*mirfade*)
1,000	pillows (*mikhadda*)
1,000	washbasins
1,000	ewers
300	stoves
1,000	candlesticks
2,000	brass objects of various kinds
1,000	belts
10,000	decorated swords
50,000	swards for the guards and pages (*ghulam*)
150,000	lances
100,000	bows
1,000	special suits of armor
10,000	helmets
20,000	breast plates
150,000	shields
4,000	special saddles
30,000	common saddles
4,000	pairs of half-boots, most of them lined with sable, mink, and other kinds of fur, with a knife and kerchief in each half-boot
4,000	pairs of socks
4,000	small tents with their appurtenances
150	marquees (large tents).

Many commodities on the first part of the list, such as precious furs from the northern parts of Central Asia and perfumes and fragrances from the Arabian Peninsula and tropical countries, arrived via the Silk Road. Silk textiles and products such as carpets, rugs, and garments certainly stand out as the largest part of his possessions.

Quite unlike Byzantium and Tang China, where the rulers restricted their subjects' consumption of governmental luxuries, the caliphs did not and could not forbid their subjects, whatever their faith, to acquire such luxuries. The life of the palace and the style of the mosques set the fashions for the Islamic world. Mas'udi says that Zubaida, a wife of Caliph Harun Al-Rashid and a fashion queen of the time, "was the first to make use of palanquins of silver, ebony and sandalwood, decorated with clasps of gold and silver, hung with *washi*, sable, brocade and red, yellow, green and blue silk. She was the first to introduce the fashion for slippers embroidered with precious stones and for candles made of ambergris—fashions which spread to the public."[11]

Palace fashions led consumers to buy the same, or at least similar, luxurious goods. Mas'udi says that Zubaida's clothes were made of "a varicolored silk called *washi*, and that a single length of this cloth designed especially for her cost 50,000 dinars."[12] Of course, not everyone was that extravagant. The ninth-century caliph Mutawakkil set another trend when he wore in public a shiny half-silk textile called *mulham*.[13] The weaving technique for mulham left the silk threads on the surface, and the cotton threads that supported the surface could only be seen on the back of the material. This was an economical way to use silk yarn, which was abundant but still more expensive than cotton or linen at that time. Probably due to its lower price, mulham became very popular all over the Islamic world in a short time. This product obviously was aimed at a market that had moderate wealth, and its popularity marked the coming of an age of much larger markets for silk textiles.

The caliphs' promotion of the consumption of silks and other luxuries did not mean they were not interested in controlling certain kinds of silk production. Like other rulers of the time, they also made use of silk textiles as a tool of governing. When the Arab conquerors first occupied Mesopotamia, Iran, Egypt, Asia Minor, and Central Asia, they found silk workshops producing textiles of various designs for secular and religious use. It was in the conquerors' financial interests to let the workshops continue to produce silks and other textiles, although they would now have to serve the needs of the new Muslim power. The tiraz system was created for that purpose.

Tiraz, a Persian word for embroidery, in Islamic culture came to refer to a silk inscription on the border of a textile. It was either woven into the fabric (as in tapestries) or embroidered onto a fabric with silk thread. It contained the Muslim profession of faith, "There is no other God but God," and the year of the caliph's or sultan's reign. As early as the Umayyad Caliphate, Islamic governments made all workshops put tiraz borders on all the textiles produced within their domain. This policy solved two problems with regard to transforming the existing silk industry into one that served the new regime. Non-Islamic silk producers often decorated their textiles with human and animal figures. Islam strongly objected to such figures, which might introduce idolatry. It also was thought that such figures mocked God's creation of living things. Islam's anti-iconic tradition created an impasse between the Muslim rulers and the conquered silk industries, whose best products were the textiles with designs of human or animal figures. Given the power of the new rulers, there was no contest, and the living figures disappeared from their subjects' silks. The tiraz borders, with their elaborate and highly artistic calligraphy, replaced the figural designs and gave rise to an Islamic textile fashion that carried both religious and political messages.

The second issue was that many Muslim consumers wondered whether or not they should wear silk, and if they did, how luxurious it could be without harming their chances of going to paradise. After much learned discussion, a general guideline for regulating textile consumption and production emerged. A robe decorated with a silk stripe that was less than two or three fingers in width or a cloth woven with a silk warp but with a weft woven of less expensive fibers would not harm the wearer's future life. Fortunately, two or three fingers' width was just enough for executing the silk inscriptions on the borders.

This limitation on silk consumption was time and place sensitive. In regions where cotton, linen, and wool were the predominant materials for textiles, such as Egypt and Mesopotamia, the tiraz was a good way to introduce silk into textile weaving. Only a small amount of silk yarn was needed to produce the decorated textiles with appropriate religious and political messages. The half-silk mulham complied with the rule and was an economical way to make beautiful textiles. In the regions where the silk weaving tradition was stronger, such as in Iran and Central Asia, tiraz were inscribed on textiles made solely from silk. And in Baghdad, the caliphs' tiraz factories made tiraz-inscribed robes of honor from whole silk.

The calligraphic designs did not entirely replace figural designs, especially outside religious architecture and furnishings. In some places, human and animal figures did continue to appear in paintings and other forms of art, including textiles. Sassanid silk styles continued to prevail in Iran, Central Asia, and China. Zandaniji silks, in particular, were still produced with unique figural designs. At the same time, Islamic inscriptions in Arabic or Persian were placed on the borders of some silk textiles or woven into the designs in the form of circles. Within the Islamic world, calligraphy was an especially well-developed art, since inscriptions and writing could be used for decoration without restrictions. The inscriptions became so artistic that on textiles and other art forms their aesthetic value became more significant than the message. Looking at those inscriptions, many people, even Muslims, could appreciate the beauty but could hardly make out the message. The combination of figures and inscriptions created a new style of Islamic textile design. Weavers sometimes wove tiny patterns of figures to form a border of a textile, actually making the figural designs a part of the tiraz border. The beauty of the tiraz textiles made them welcome not only in the markets of Islamic countries but also in other regions, including Christian Europe.

The tiraz, like coinage, was one of the most efficient means of communication between Islamic rulers and their subjects. These inscriptions became a kind of early trademark, giving information about the textile's producer, provenance, and date of production. Except for the factories that produced robes of honor for the caliphs, most tiraz factories were not government run, but producers did need a license. The license system never restricted silk production but gave the government control over tiraz as a tool of propaganda and over quality of products from various regions. And by the late Abbasid Caliphate, silk materials were so abundant that most tiraz inscriptions were on silk textiles.

Muslims were probably the first people outside China who truly mastered the essential technologies of sericulture, and most important, the making of long filaments, which were mandatory for fine textiles. The Byzantines had tried earlier, but it took them longer to succeed. After Justinian started the effort, a special office called the Kommerki-arior was in charge of sericulture. However, as Byzantine weavers wove mostly the heavy type of brocade or tapestry, it is not clear whether they knew how to make long filaments. At any rate, even if the Byzantine sericulture and filature did fully develop to the extent that it could supply its own silk looms, it was soon lost to the Islamic conquests.

Gradually, from the seventh century on, the Byzantines lost many of the lands planted with mulberry trees to the Arabs. Fortunately for the Byzantine silk industry, the Arabs who possessed these lands needed the profits they made by selling the silk yarn outside their own perimeters. The function of the Byzantine Kommerkiarior changed from developing sericulture to managing the importation of silk yarn from Islamic countries.[14] Given the evidence accumulated so far, it appears that the long filament technology practiced in China did not appear in other silk-producing countries prior to the mid-eighth century. Judging by all the surviving samples that have been found outside Iran, Sassanid Persia made only the heaviest types of silk, which do not require long strands of silk. As for Central Asia and India, Chinese pilgrims in the early seventh century observed that the silk yarn produced there was also made with the shorter type of fiber. Apparently this situation did not change until 751, when an Islamic army rode east to meet the Tang army in Central Asia.

In the eighth century, Tang military power was predominant in much of Central Asia. However, when Gao Xianzhi, the Chinese military commander in Central Asia, became involved in a conflict with the oasis state of Tashkent (in present-day Uzbekistan), it asked for help from the newly established Abbasid Caliphate in Baghdad. The two armies met at the Talas River (where it crosses the border between Kyrgyzstan and Kazakhstan), where the Islamic army defeated the Tang forces of General Gao. The Muslims took many prisoners of war, including Chinese artisans skilful in painting and weaving. This happened at the same time that the new caliphate was building its new capital, Baghdad. One of the prisoners, a scholar named Du Huan (mid-eighth century), remained in the Islamic lands for eleven years and left a description of the Islamic religion and urban life in the caliphate; unfortunately only fragments, quoted in his brother Du You's history book, have survived. Du Huan admired the prosperity of the Arab empire: "Every thing produced from the earth is available there. Carts carry countless goods to markets, where every thing is available and cheap. Brocade, embroidered silks, pearls, and other gems are displayed all over markets and street shops."[15] He met several Chinese artisans who were goldsmiths, silversmiths, painters, and weavers specializing in various silk textiles. He mentioned their names, professions, and homelands in China. Apparently, Chinese workers were participating in the construction of Baghdad and the Abbasid Empire. Soon after the battle at Talas, mulberry trees as a commercial crop spread all the way from Central Asia to North Africa and southern Spain. Sericulture, including the skill of drawing long filaments from the silk cocoons, then became a mature technology well known to Muslim artisans.

By the end of the ninth century, silk yarn from Islamic countries became so abundant that Muslim traders started to export some of their production to the Byzantine market. By this time, the Byzantine government no longer monopolized silk materials. The *Book of the Eparch* lists separate rules for the merchants who imported manufactured silks from Syria and Baghdad, for those who imported raw silk, and for artisans who worked with the raw silk. Merchants who imported silks from various Islamic areas, whether they were Byzantines or Muslims, as well as the people who dealt in manufactured textiles or silk materials, were in the city of Constantinople all year round and were organized into guilds.[16] The government no longer controlled all the imported silks but instead regulated the guilds.

The Byzantine state controlled the dyers' guild more strictly than the silk guilds. Any dyer who dared to use even a tiny amount of Tyrian purple dye risked having his hands cut off. This was not a problem for the Muslim merchants, since Muslims in general did not care for the color purple and thought Byzantine rulers' fondness for it was rather odd. The Islamic scholar and traveler Ibn Khordâdhbeh (825–912) describes the Byzantine emperor as wearing a kind of shiny blackish-purple robe called "al-furfir," or purple. He was amazed that the emperor prohibited his subjects from wearing purple and astonished at the order that whoever dared to do so would have his head cut off.[17] This essential status marker in the Byzantine Empire and the Christian world was meaningless to the merchants coming from Islamic cultures.

Christians, however, loved both silks and purple dye. Western European Christians were eager to buy silks for their churches, liturgical rituals, and vestments. The silk textiles produced in the Islamic countries, both plain and figured, were welcomed. As Muslim artisans neither dyed the silk purple nor wove figures of Christian saints, using the imported silks for religious purposes sometimes required further processing. Lacking the technology of complicated looms for making figured silks, devout Christians resorted to embroidery, which could produce the desired patterns with simple needles. The papacy in Rome set up a workshop for embroidering figures of saints on silk textiles in gold. Having a piece of silk embroidered with the image of the patron saint of a particular church and then granting the piece to that church demonstrated the pope's true concern for that particular parish. Plain silk, whether from Islamic countries or further east, came to supplement the limited supply of the elaborate Byzantine silks to the

In this fifteenth-century Italian painting, the Virgin Mary wears a purple cloak with a golden border embroidered with words. Tiraz, or borders of textiles embroidered in Arabic with silk threads, were standard for all textiles in Islamic countries and became highly regarded fabrics in Christian countries, too, as a result of Silk Road commerce. Renaissance painters innocently adopted this style for Mary. © National Gallery, London / Art Resource, NY churches in western Europe, and this silk, too, could be covered with embroidery.

Western Europeans also imported exquisite silk textiles that had been made in the Islamic countries. Figured silk textiles, such as the Zandaniji from Bukhara, often found their way to Christian churches in Europe. Nevertheless, the most abundant silk textiles from Islamic regions were tiraz, which seem to have been very popular among the Christians. Images of Christ and Mary in church paintings and on stained glass often show these figures wearing purple robes with tiraz borders. The Christian artists who designed those portraits and the people who wore tiraz silk clothing were apparently unaware of the Islamic religious messages in the inscriptions. As noted, the inscriptions were so stylized for aesthetic purposes that even most Muslims could hardly read them. The purple robes with tiraz borders were most likely products of Christian artists' imaginations, since Muslim weavers never made purple silks. When imagining fitting vestments for Christ and the saints, these artists apparently borrowed the idea of the color purple from Byzantium and combined it with the borders on the popular tiraz textiles. There is no doubt that Islamic traders left their own homelands and crossed the borders of their religions' domains in order to sell their products all over Eurasia.

By the tenth century, efficient Islamic trading networks extended across most of Eurasia as well as North Africa and Africa's eastern coast, and to some locations in West Africa. Ironically, it was the weakening of the Abbasid Caliphate and the disintegration of the imperial structure that sped up the propagation of Islam to areas remote from the center of the empire. In the Mediterranean, the Shiite Fatimid Caliphate (909–1171), which was based in Egypt, stretched westward along North Africa's Mediterranean coast and also encompassed the eastern coast of the Mediterranean and western Arabia, the homeland of Islam. In addition, an Ummayad caliphate had ruled southern Spain. The old Semitic language- and Persian-speaking lands, the core region of Islamic culture under the Abbasids, split into several smaller states. The Iranian Buyids (932–1062), who were Shiites, ruled over Baghdad and retained the Abbasid caliphs as puppets. On the eastern part of the Iranian plateau and in nearby Afghanistan, the Samanids (819–1005) maintained a nominal loyalty to the Abbasids but had in fact long been autonomous in local affairs. These regional powers, from Spain to Egypt to Central Asia, continued the tradition of patronizing Islamic art and learning. Cairo, as the capital of the Fatimids, became another center of Islamic culture, second only to Baghdad. In the eastern part of the Islamic world,

Persian became the cultural and religious language of the Muslims and eventually spread throughout an area much larger than the territory of any previous Persian empire. Most of the population living in these lands of ancient civilizations now converted to Islam.

Meanwhile, the drama of conflict and mutual dependence between the nomads on the steppe and the sedentary agricultural states continued. In the sixth century, the Turkish tribes had come to power on China's northern border. They began expanding westward, where they would have a profound impact on the post-Abbasid Islamic political structures in the eastern part of what had been the Abbasid Empire, in large part due to the military weakness of the successor states that followed the breakdown of Abbasid power. These states—under the rule of the Buyids, the Samanids, and others—discarded the previously effective central administration of the Abbasid Caliphate and paid their own military commanders in land grants. This system encouraged the growth of a military elite who soon wielded tremendous power over civilian authorities. As the Turkish population migrated eastward, they joined these armies and converted to Islam. First the Samanids and then the Buyids used Turkish slaves as soldiers in their armies. Thanks to their military abilities, many of these former slaves rose quickly through the ranks, and many became commanders. In 999, the Turkish slaves who garrisoned the eastern rim of the Samanid domain overthrew their masters and established the Ghaznavid state. The Ghaznavid ruler, Mahmud, then pillaged northwestern India annually to obtain booty that enabled him to build mosques and libraries in Ghazni. He hoped to receive an honorary title from the caliph of Baghdad so that he could establish himself as a pan-Islamic leader. However, the glory of the Ghaznavids turned out to be temporary. A fresh wave of Turkish migration from the eastern end of the steppe, the Seljuk Turks, came to the rescue of the fractured Islamic regime.

In 1055 these Turks entered Baghdad, where they replaced the Shiite Buyids and ostensibly served as Sunni patrons of the caliph. Seljuk power then extended across most of what is now Turkey at the expense of Byzantium, all the way to the eastern coast of the Mediterranean, at great cost to the Fatimids of Egypt. Nonetheless, the Seljuk Empire was also short-lived; after the death of Malik Shah in 1071, it started to disintegrate. Nevertheless, for some two hundred years thereafter, until the Mongol conquests of the thirteenth century, various Turkish Islamic regimes held sway over lands that stretched all the way from the Amu River in Central Asia to the eastern Mediterranean coast. The first intrusions of the Turks onto the tilled lands were as destructive as those of their nomadic predecessors. Nevertheless, they quickly became patrons of Islamic high cultures, in order to enhance their own status. In particular, Islamic architecture became the dominant landmark of Turkish-occupied Central Asia. Although the Arab army had conquered the western part of Central Asia a couple of centuries earlier, the conversion of the local population to Islam had been quite slow in this region. Only after the Islamic Turks ruled both the steppe and the oases did the landscape became Islamic.

Muslim traders soon traveled wherever there were Islamic rulers in power as well as to regions far beyond. Not surprisingly, they soon took over the bulk of the trade on the Silk Road, while Islamic institutions, like the Buddhist ones before them, established themselves on all the major trade routes. Both mosques and the tombs of Islamic saints became places where weary travelers could stop and rest. Islamic patrons built hostels, known as caravanserai, that accommodated both people and beasts of burden. In addition, the Seljuk Turks who controlled the western part of the Silk Road offered the traders a special guarantee of safety. The government assured their financial security by paying compensation out of the state treasury for any loss caused by robbery. The Turkish authorities, whether the unified Seljuk sultanate or independent amirs, also built fortified caravanserais that provided food, fodder, and lodging for the travelers at intervals of one day's journey apart all along the trade routes.

Thus, Islamic institutions provided the infrastructure for a large section of the Silk Road. Even in places where Islam was not dominant, such as India, China, and the Byzantine Empire, Islamic religious institutions hosted Muslim travelers and traders. Although the Islamic world was divided into many political units and differing sects, hostilities between rulers and religious leaders were no hindrance to travelers, pilgrims, or traders. Many Islamic scholars who traveled these routes have left detailed and accurate records of the various peoples of Eurasia and Africa during this time. From their writings, we learn that the Islamic scholars were always welcomed and taken care of by the local religious institutions and trading communities. Scholars also sought patronage from Turkish sultans and amirs, who sponsored the construction of mosques and libraries. Islamic architecture in Central Asian cities such as Bukhara and Samarkand was represented by new landmarks of the Silk Road.

The Mongols caused so much damage during the thirteenth century that very few cultural remains survive on the Central Asian Silk Road from the early Islamic period. Other cultural legacies, such as linguistic changes, are more obvious. The Persian tongue in particular, with some Arabic vocabulary added in, spread eastward, far from its homeland, along with Islam, and is now an official Islamic language. Soon after the Arab conquests in Central Asia, Persian replaced Sogdian as the lingua franca on the Silk Road. The early Islamic conquests also damaged some of the Buddhist and Sogdian commercial networks; indeed, cities such as Samarkand and Bukhara became centers of Islamic culture. Sogdians quickly adapted to the political situation by joining the new faith and accommodating the new powers. Mosques rose in Sogdian cities, and the Islamic financial system was extended all the way from the Middle East to Central Asia. Unfortunately, the Mongols destroyed all the Islamic architecture built during this period. We can only try to imagine the cities, markets, mosques, and citadels described by early Islamic geographers.

The mass production and trade of textiles grew during the Islamic period. After the Abbasid Caliphate and its successor states encouraged the tiraz system and the spread of sericulture, the coming of the Turkish Islamic culture on the Silk Road added another dimension to the textile industry: the production of carpets, draperies and upholstery. Once the nomads began living in settled societies, these heavy textiles that were an essential part of their tent culture became part of their furniture. Rugs and tapestries are yet another example of the linkage of material culture with technology and of the interaction between nomadic and sedentary societies. The high point in the development of silk and wool tapestries and rugs, from the Middle East to Central Asia, came after the Islamic Turks extended their rule from Central Asia to Baghdad, Egypt, and southern Europe. However, very few rugs and carpets remain from this period; almost all of the rugs and carpets in today's museums were produced after the Mongol conquests.

The only significant cultural remains that date to the years when Islamic patronage dominated the Silk Road are tiraz and other silk textiles made under Islamic auspices that found their way to churches and cathedrals in Europe, where they escaped the thirteenth-century Mongol conquests. The Zandaniji textiles produced in the vicinity of Bukhara during the Islamic era survived mostly in European churches.

Over the years of Turkish rule, the world changed. Silk yarn became no longer a rare commodity but a standard of exchange from the Mediterranean to the South China Sea. As agriculture developed in western Europe, South Asia, China, and Japan, their growing populations demanded more goods for consumption. The demands of this new, larger market overwhelmed the traditional long-distance trade that had kept royal courts and religious institutions in luxuries. In addition, traders came to prefer sea routes due to the improvement of ship building and navigation technology. A growing sector of the international trade consisted of heavy bulk goods, such as porcelain and tea. Camels and horses were no longer profitable means of transportation.

CHAPTER 6

The Mongols and the Twilight of the Silk Road

Like many of their steppe predecessors, Mongols of the thirteenth century destroyed almost all the facilities along the trade routes during their initial conquests. And, like their predecessors, they subsequently became patrons of trade and sponsors of religious activities all along the routes that passed through the lands they conquered. Genghis Khan lavishly wrote: "As my quiver bearers are black like a thick forest and [my] wives, spouses [*sic*] and daughters glitter and sparkle like a red hot fire, my desire and intention for all is such: to delight their mouths with the sweetness of the sugar of benevolence, to adorn them front and back, top and bottom, with garments of gold brocade, to sit them on fluid paced mounts, to give them pure and delicious water to drink, to provide verdant pastures for their herds."[1]

Mongol rulers recruited local traders, artisans, and scholars immediately after every conquest to help them manage their empire, and especially to construct their capital on the steppe, in what is now central Mongolia. For a century or so the Central Asian steppe was once again the link between Europe and China, as Mongol conquerors facilitated commercial and cultural exchanges on the Eurasian land routes. But the growing sea trade would change all that.

Genghis Khan was born during China's Song Dynasty (960–1279). At that time, China had a robust economy, with a large export sector supplying foreign demand. Silk yarn and silk textiles were still important exports, even though their availability outside China was increasing due to the spread of production techniques. Increased quantities of spices and incense, no longer used just for cooking and rituals, but now also for medicinal properties, were also being traded from the Arabian Peninsula as well as Southeast and South Asia. Agricultural development had also led to population increases in Eurasia and Africa, thereby increasing the demand for local and imported commodities.

In addition to China's traditional products, tea and porcelain drinking vessels associated with tea drinking, as well as porcelain dishes, enjoyed an international boom. Tea was especially popular among the

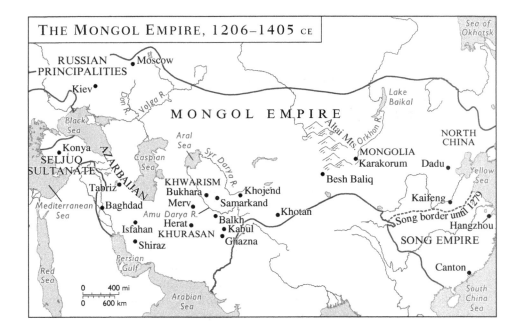

THE MONGOL EMPIRE, 1206–1405 CE

nomads. Indeed, it was so popular that the tea-horse trade had replaced the old silk-horse trade on the northern borders of the Song Empire. Tea was also a favorite in Japan and the Islamic countries. Although porcelain ware was related to the tea culture, it was also independently significant. It, too, contributed to the growth in the maritime trade, since its relative fragility meant that it had to be packed in bulky and heavy containers, and its transport by ships was much more efficient than by caravans. It was in large part due to the demand for porcelain that countries all along the coasts of the Indian Ocean and the western Pacific became involved in the maritime trade.

Affluent as it was, Song China faced the usual problems with nomads expanding from the north. In the middle of the tenth century, the Qidan nomads, who were originally from the Mongolian steppe, established a state called Liao and expanded across present-day northeast China. In this vast area of grasslands, forests, and river basins, the Liao Empire embraced tribes of nomads, hunters, fishers, and farmers. The relationship of the Liao state to Song China was complicated; sometimes the Liao were at peace with the Song court and sometimes at war. Eventually, the Liao established their southern border to include the area around modern Beijing, where they established a second capital within what had been the boundaries of the Song Empire.

A nomadic hunting-gathering tribe called the Nüzhen arose in the northeastern part of the Liao Empire while it was settling in north China and fighting the Song army. By 1120, the Nüzhen had conquered all of the Liao Empire and transformed their tribal structure into a state known as the Jin, which then proceeded to pursue the Song court all the way south to the Yangzi River Valley. To make matters worse for the Song state, at the same time it was confronting the Jin army in central China, another nomadic people, the Mongols, arose on the northern horizon. By the 1210s, Genghis Khan had unified numerous tribes on the Mongolian steppe and conquered the Jin, including the Beijing region. He started to dream about decorating his tents and his women with gold and silk. But he had no intention of settling down on the conquered agricultural lands or of making himself an emperor of China. Instead, he established his capital at Karakorum, at the very center of the Mongolian steppe.

Genghis Khan began to build his state by establishing a law code, appointing judges for civil and criminal cases, and employing a Turkic-speaking scholar to invent a script for the Mongolian language, which until then had not been written. Genghis also realized that the steppe religion of heaven worship would not serve the large empire he was in the process of founding. In 1218, he summoned Yelü Chucai, a scholar-official who had served the Jin court, to his imperial court, which was housed in a tent, to discuss affairs of state and religion. Yelü Chucai had been born into an aristocratic lineage of the Qidan and had become a Buddhist and Confucian while serving the Jin regime. He offered much good advice to Genghis and his successors. Indeed, he sometimes risked his career as well as his life when his opinions differed from those of the Mongol elite. Yelü Chucai by and large succeeded in persuading the Mongols to preserve agriculture in the parts of their empire where it was already flourishing, instead of trying to change all the lands they controlled into pastures for horses and sheep.

Genghis Khan was eager to attract to his steppe court the merchants who delivered the prestigious goods that came from the agricultural societies. He had guards patrol the major routes to guarantee the safety of travelers and goods destined for Karakorum. News of the demand for such goods and the possibility of large profits from them spread all over Central Asia, and traders headed eastward to Karakorum. Three merchants from Bukhara in Transoxiana, an area that encompassed the Amu and Syr rivers as they flowed westward into the Aral Sea, brought many exquisite textiles—gold-embroidered fabrics, cotton, and Zandaniji silk—together with other goods to the court of the khan.[2] Genghis not only paid the merchants handsomely in gold but also ordered his wives, daughters, and commanders to employ Muslim traders to help them spend their gold allotments taken as booty for the luxury silk and other textiles. Entrusted with gold and silver ingots, the recruited Muslim traders could follow the Bukhara merchants home to Khwarazmshah, the Islamic state that ruled a large portion of Central Asia, including Transoxiana.

Genghis sent out an official delegation with a letter to the sultan of Khwarazmshah with this message: "Merchants from your country have come among us, and we have sent them back in the manner that you shall hear. And we have likewise dispatched to your country in their company a group of merchants in order that they may acquire the wondrous wares of those regions; and that henceforth the abscess of evil thought may be lanced by the improvement of relations and agreements between us, and the pus of sedition and rebellion removed."[3] Indeed, the hometowns of Genghis's envoys, Mahmud Khwarazmi (the last name means he was from Khwarazm), Ali Khwajah Bukhari (from Bukhara), and Yusuf Kanka Utrari (from Utrar) had all been encompassed within the realm of Khwarazmshah.[4] The sultan, though hesitant, agreed to sign a treaty with the Mongols. Nevertheless, for reasons unknown, when the Mongolian caravan, headed by the Muslim merchants, arrived at Utrar, one of Khwarazmshah's frontier garrison posts, the local governor had the delegation of about one hundred members killed and their goods confiscated. Genghis, outraged, still intended to negotiate with the sultan and sent another ambassador, who was supposed to demand the extradition of the offending governor to the Mongols. However, the governor was the sultan's uncle. The sultan refused the demand and had the second ambassador from Genghis executed as well. According to several historians of the period, this incident ignited the first Mongol military expedition against the powers to his west.

Yelü Chucai, who had arrived at the court of Genghis in 1218, about the same time as the massacre took place in Utrar, became the Mongol ruler's confidant and accompanied him on the western expedition against the sultan of Khwarazmshah. He stayed with the Mongol army for the entire expedition, which returned from the west in 1224. Three years later, when Yelü Chucai visited Yan, his homeland in the vicinity of modern Beijing, he wrote a small book describing the "Western Region" he had observed. He gives absolutely no account of the battles or their aftermath and confines his account to a description of the mountains, rivers, cities, and products available along the routes the Mongol expedition took. "When the army passed the Golden Mountain in the midsummer, snowflakes blew around the mountain peaks and ice accumulated to a thousand *chi* deep. The khan ordered the soldiers to cut the ice to pave a road for the troops to cross. There were hundreds and thousands of springs in the Golden Mountain. Pines and junipers grew so tall they almost touched the sky; flowers and grass covered the valleys."[5] Judging from his narrative, the Mongol army under Genghis Khan crossed the Altai Mountains (the location of "Golden Mountain"; in what is now western Mongolia) and then marched past the eastern foothills of the Tianshan Mountains. Yelü Chucai also mentions two cities, Gaochang in the Turfan area and Khotan on the southern rim of the Takla Makan Desert, inside the Tarim Basin, and points out that both were well known during Tang times. After the expedition crosses the Talas River and enters the territory of Khwarazmshah, his records become much more detailed. He writes that Khojend produced huge pomegranates, and remarks that the watermelons in Bap were so big that a donkey could carry only two. He also mentions the city of Utrar, where the governor had killed Genghis Khan's delegation and more than one hundred merchants.

Samarkand, he writes, was the most beautiful city of all. It was located in a very fertile land, and "it was surrounded by numerous gardens. Every household had a garden, and all the gardens were well designed, with canals and water fountains that supplied water to round or square-shaped ponds. The landscape included rows of willows and cypress trees, and peach and plum orchards were shoulder to shoulder.... In the dry summer, water was lifted from the river for irrigation. The grape wine was excellent."[6] He was so impressed by this beautiful city that he wrote several poems in praise of it.

Yelü Chucai does not describe the bloody battle and subsequent miserable surrender of Samarkand, which was recorded in several other sources. He did not see the city before the battle, since he was riding with the Mongol army; what he describes must have been what he saw after the battle was over. He also mentions several other old Silk Road cities in this region such as Bukhara, Balkh, or Bactra (now in Afghanistan), and Termez on the Amu River (Tuan), which were all still flourishing. He noticed that in Termez there was plenty of lacquerware in the market. Lacquerware was a Chinese product and a popular commodity in the Silk Road trade. What is most interesting about the lacquerware Yelü Chucai saw is that it dated not to the Song but to the previous Tang Empire, which indicates that it was more than three hundred years old. The vessels all carried the inscription "Chang'an" (the name of the Tang capital), which during the Tang Empire had served as a trademark for items made in the capital.[7] It seems that this section of the Silk Road had sustained its economy under the Turkish Islamic regime of Khwarazmshah but may have lost its commercial ties with China after the fall of the Tang in the early tenth century. Even after the destruction wrought by the Mongol conquests in Khwarazmshah, the resilience of these cities, which were already more than a thousand years old, continued to sustain them as regional cultural and economic centers until modern times.

The Mongol conquest of Khwarazmshah revitalized the Transoxiana region as the hinge between the eastern and western parts of Eurasia. From this region, Genghis Khan and his successors recruited both skilled craftsmen and well-educated civil servants to help build their empire. Ata-Malik Juvaini (ca. 1226–83), the historian of Genghis Khan's reign, described the Mongols' process of recruiting supporters after they besieged Samarkand:

> On the third day…the greater part of the Mongols entered the town, and the men and women in groups of a hundred were driven out into the open in the charge of Mongol soldiers; only the *cadi* [Muslim judges] and the *Shaikh-al Islam* [Muslim nobles] together with such as had some connection with them and stood under their protection were exempted from leaving the town. More than fifty thousand people were counted who remained under such protection.[8]

The first step was to separate out the Islamic religious leaders and scholars and their protégés, so as to save them from slaughter and forced conscription. The next day, after the citadel fell and was burned to the ground and the military forces of the sultan were destroyed,

> the people who had escaped from beneath the sword were numbered; thirty thousand of them were chosen for their craftsmanship, and these Genghis Khan distributed amongst his sons and kinsmen, while the like number were selected from the youthful and valiant to form a levy. With regard to the remainders, who obtained permission to return into the town…he imposed [a ransom of] two hundred thousand dinars…and deputed the collection of this sum to…the chief officials of Samarkand. He then appointed several persons to be *shahnas* [agents to collect tribute] from the town and took some of the levies with him to Khorasan, while the others he sent to Khorazm [Khwarism] with his sons. And afterwards, several times in succession levies were raised in Samarkand and few only were exempted there from; and for this reason complete ruin overran the country.[9]

Fine craftsmen were spared from the slaughter but torn from their homeland and carried off to Mongolia, where they were distributed among the Mongol princes and princesses to weave silk brocade and tapestries and to make gold jewelry and other beautiful objects. In addition, in accord with Yelü Chucai's advice, the great khan allowed the nonskilled residents who had survived the battles to continue to live in the city, so long as they paid taxes and served as conscripts.

Genghis Khan set an example for his successors in employing Muslim soldiers, traders, scholars, and craftsmen. Soon after the campaign, many talented people from the Transoxiana region found their way to high positions in various Mongol regimes. In Khwarazmshah, when Genghis Khan's army was marching into the region of Bukhara, Sayyid Ajall Omer Shams Al-Din, a powerful and respected man of that city, went out to meet the Mongol chief with a thousand cavalrymen, whom he offered to the khan. He was soon posted to strategically important positions, including, among others, governor of Yanjing (modern Beijing). Sayyid Ajall, who was both an excellent military commander and a skillful administrator, successfully waged numerous campaigns in China, including the critical final battle at Xiangfan, the Song Dynasty's last stronghold on the Yangzi River. He managed to restore order and increase the taxable population and thus revenue in several provinces. His political savvy saved him from disasters caused by the jealousies among his Mongol colleagues that often brought misfortune on the regime's non-Mongol staff.

Most of the Muslims from what had been Khwarazmshah who entered the service of the Mongol rulers were financial officials and administrators, including a number of outstanding scholars. Juvaini, the aforementioned historian who composed his history of "the world conqueror" while living in Karakorum, the conqueror's own capital, would become the governor of Mongolian-controlled Baghdad later in his career. His homeland in Khorasan was within the realm of Khwarazmshah when Genghis Khan conquered it. During the conquest, his grandfather was in the service of the sultan of Khwarazmshah and accompanied his lord as he fled the Mongols. His father, however, Baha-ad-Din, was enrolled in service to the Mongols as a financial administrator.[10] Juvaini's emotionless and candid narrative of the bloody careers of his Mongol overlords presents a sharp contrast to Yelü Chucai's subtle dodge of any such scenes in his memoir. Both had successful, if turbulent, careers under the Mongol regimes. Juvaini, Yelü Chucai, Sayyid Ajall, and the distinguished Persian scholar Rashid al-Din, as well as numerous other outstanding individuals from the conquered lands, lent their talents to the Mongols and made the Mongolian khanates functional states.

More than any other population, Muslim officials from Khwarazmshah gained the trust of the Mongol rulers, due in large part to their bureaucratic and financial skills. In 1271, the great khan Khubilai proclaimed himself emperor of the Chinese-style Yuan Empire and adopted Tibetan Buddhism as the state religion, yet even there Muslim officials continued to hold some of the highest positions, outranked by only the highest-ranking Mongols. Some used their power wisely and efficiently, for example Sayyid Ajall, who governed Yunnan (in what is now the southwestern corner of China). Early in their effort to conquer the southern part of China, the Mongols had, for strategic reasons, also conquered Yunnan. Southern Chinese resistance to the Mongols was so strong and the terrain there so defensible against cavalries that the conquest took from 1253 until 1279. Yunnan posed a serious challenge to the Mongolian-Chinese administration. It was located in a mountainous, subtropical forest and was home to many distinct ethnic groups. For more than a millennium, the peoples of this region had successfully blocked any Chinese influence within their bounds. Sayyid Ajall, a Muslim from Khwarazmshah, nevertheless managed to introduce both irrigation agriculture and Confucian education into this area without provoking rebellions.[11] Even now, seven and a half centuries later, the local peoples of Yunnan well remember his benevolent administration.

Other Muslim officials, such as the infamous Ahmad, who also came from the Transoxiana region, gained Khubilai's utmost trust but abused their power so as to amass personal wealth. Ahmad survived several investigations, and only after he was killed by a group of rebels did the emperor realize that he had committed such crimes.[12]

Muslim merchants, who were even more numerous than the Muslim scholar-officials, also lent essential assistance to the Mongol rulers. Genghis Khan, in particular, admired and trusted merchants, thinking they had to be both brave and smart to successfully bring all their exotic goods to his tent-covered court. In the confrontation with Khwarazmshah, merchants of the Transoxiana region worked with both the Muslim sultan and the Mongol khan. Both the great khan and his retinue entrusted their gold and silver ingots to the Muslim traders to make purchases on their behalf. Genghis Khan set the example of employing Muslim traders as contractors, or *ortog*, a word of Turkic origin meaning "partner."[13] These merchant contractors traveled all around the Mongolian-controlled realms with certificates issued by the princes and nobles indicating that they were acquiring goods for these powerful customers. In order to protect the safe arrival of gold brocade and other silk and woolen textiles for their clothing and tents, Genghis Khan and his successors carefully garrisoned the routes leading to Karakorum to prevent robberies. However, if a caravan was robbed anyway and the robbers escaped with their loot, the local population was held responsible for the loss and forced to compensate the traders.[14] Innocent residents were often harassed for something they did not do. The Muslim ortogs may have been jewels in the eyes of the Mongol ruling elite, but they were sometimes a cause of devastation for these rulers' subjects.

After the death of Genghis Khan in 1227, the Mongol princes born to his principal wife divided the empire into four khanates. Muslim officials and merchants became even more important to the sons than they had been to their father. In the Yuan Empire (China) and the Il Khanate (Iran), the Mongols were ruling lands that depended on agriculture, with which they had little previous experience, and in both places, they tended to make use of various local traditions to build up a variety of bureaucratic systems. Even though the Yuan rulers converted to Tibetan Buddhism and the Il khans eventually converted to Islam, these two khanates maintained good relations and had frequent exchanges of envoys and goods. In contrast, the lands held by the Chaghatai Khanate in Central Asia and the Golden Horde on the southern Russian steppe had relatively little agriculture, except in the places with oases. Among the khanates and within each of them, it was not unusual for Genghis's successors, following the precedent set by their father, to employ Muslim merchants as tax collectors for their master-partners. These merchant-contractors annoyed and harassed hard-pressed taxpayers.

In China, the Muslim tax collectors' pretensions of simply serving their Mongol masters were especially irritating because the Yuan government had granted them a privileged status. In order to control their rebellious Chinese subjects, the Yuan rulers had registered the population and then divided them into four hierarchical categories. All Mongols, rich or poor, capable or derelict, were in the highest rank, and thus eligible for important governmental positions. Foreigners, such as the Muslims and the Nestorian Christians, were in the second-highest category, and some of them became high-level commanders and administrators in the government. Even though the Nestorian Christians were easily accepted in China at that time, most of the high-ranking positions were held by Muslims, often those with roots in the Transoxiana region. The northern Chinese, who had surrendered to Mongol rule earlier than the southerners, were in the third rank. The southern Chinese, who had resisted the

Mongol conquest for more than half a century, were put in the lowest social category to prevent them from undermining the regime.

Whereas Mongol troops garrisoned cities and towns and enforced curfews, it was a shrewd move for the rulers of the Yuan Empire to assign the hard job of collecting taxes to Muslim traders. If farmers could not pay all their taxes during crop failures, they had to borrow money from Muslim moneylenders at usurious rates or faced the possibility of arrest for nonpayment. From the point of view of the suffering populace, the Muslim traders and moneylenders were even more hateful than their ruthless Mongol masters.

The Mongol rulers were always inclined to trust the Muslim traders because they needed traders. Genghis's Mongol followers had faith in him because he brought them tremendous material wealth and changed their lives fundamentally. According to Juvaini, the Mongols had once worn clothing made from the skins of dogs and mice, eaten the flesh of those animals as well as nuts from the trees, and drunk a wine made from mares' milk. The privilege of a chief had been no more than a pair of iron stirrups. Genghis Khan brought them a life wherein they wore silk and brocade, ate the meats of their choice, and drank imported grape wine.[15] This life of paradise on the steppe depended on a constant supply of products from sedentary agricultural societies—no problem for the great khan, who had more than enough gold and silver loot with which to purchase such luxuries. Most likely in his later years Genghis Khan achieved his dream of dressing his entire retinue in clothes made of gold-threaded brocade.

Several varieties of gold brocade achieved popularity during the years of the Mongols' power. They most treasured *nasij*, a patterned silk textile heavily tapestried with gold-wrapped threads. In fact, the Mongols used this golden silk to create a new fashion that can still be seen today, almost a millennium later. They were the first to turn fur robes and jackets inside out, using the fur as the lining and the gold-covered silk as the shell. Many people still believe fur coats are actually warmer when made this way, even without a silk cover.

Silk brocades made with gold-wrapped threads were not a new product during the days of Genghis Khan. Their origin dates to the golden age of silk textile industries in Sassanid Iran and Tang China. Thereafter, they continued to develop even after Islamic power extended westward across North Africa to Spain and eastward into Central Asia. During their conquests, the Mongols not only snatched these glittering textiles as part of their booty but also had their ortogs purchase them. Since Genghis Khan, the empire's founder, spent most of his time away from Karakorum on

In this page from The Great Mongol Shahnama (Book of Kings), *Bahram Gur, an ancient Iranian hero, is depicted wearing a bright silk robe, as commonly seen in Mongol times. Mongol rulers became patrons of culture and art. This lavishly illustrated copy of the Iranian classical work was made in Tabriz, the capital of the Il Khanate, around the 1330s.* Arthur M. Sackler Gallery, Smithsonian Institution, Washington, D.C.: Purchase-Smithsonian Unrestricted Trust Funds, Smithsonian Collections Acquisition Program, and Dr. Arthur M. Sackler, S1986.103a-b

various expeditions, he did not have much time to build a splendid political center at his capital. Only after he died and his third son, Ogodei, was chosen as the next great khan came the buildup of wealth arriving from the conquered lands at the tent city of Karakorum.

Karakorum was located on the Orkhon River in central Mongolia, far from any commercial depots or agricultural lands. To transform it into an impressive political center, Ogodei had thousands of artisans relocated there, mostly from Transoxiana and China. At least five hundred carts per day arrived at the site, just to supply the building materials and the food for the craftsmen and servants, as well as the rulers themselves.[16] Thus, the Silk Road during the time of Mongol ascendancy was essentially the steppe routes that carried silks and other goods from Iran, Transoxiana, and China to Karakorum. This Silk Road, however, was unique in that the purchasers of the silks and other fine goods frequently paid for them with the booty they had carried home from foreign conquests.

At Karakorum, Chinese and Muslim artisans built a tent city at the center of a large walled garden that had four gates. The city housed a palatial tent, erected by Chinese workers, which included the great khan's throne room. Here he entertained all his princes, nobles, and foreign guests twice a year. He displayed his authority to the world with a series of banquets that could last an entire month. In the spring Ogodei lived in a palace designed and built by Muslim artisans, "a very tall castle filled with all kinds of many-colored, jewel-studded embroideries and carpets," according to Juvaini.[17] For the summer, Chinese workers built a pavilion at a cool site in the mountains. Though this pavilion was built in a Chinese style, structurally it was a white felt tent supported by a wooden lattice and covered with gold-embroidered silk textiles.[18] Muslim artisans and their Chinese counterparts competed with each other in showing off their skills and aesthetic talents in order to gain favor with the Mongol ruler.

Ogodei transported workers from the Transoxiana region and China to build the exquisite tent structures, but the silk textiles could not be made in Mongolia because it is impossible to establish sericulture in the climate there. The tents and clothing, made of gold brocade or gold embroidery, had to be imported. The Mongols had a strong desire for both Chinese- and Persian-style golden silk textiles, but their favorite was the nasij woven in Iran and Transoxiana. This preference was most likely due to the different ways the gold was integrated into the textile. In Tang silks, the gold thread was made by gilding thin strips of paper and then wrapping them around the silk threads. The gold threads in Chinese brocades take on the flat shape of the paper, so they do not perfectly match the nongold silk threads. In contrast, the Persians and the artisans in the Transoxiana region managed to find a way to create golden silk threads that were not flat and could be used for both tapestry and embroidery. In the eyes of the Mongols, the Chinese golden silks were less beautiful than the Persian ones.

Ogodei also relocated textile artisans from Transoxiana to northern China. After Ogodei became great khan, he also moved some of the artisans collected by Genghis Khan closer to his own capital. He ordered Hasanna, one of Genghis Khan's generals, back to Samarkand in order to relocate 3,000 households of textile artisans to Xunmalin, a locale on the border of modern Shanxi and Hebei provinces in northern China. A town was created in the foothills just inside the Great Wall where these artisans wove textiles and made wine for the Mongol rulers. Whether wine was an original goal of the project is unclear, but once the artisans from Samarkand arrived, they built gardens in the fashion of their homeland and planted vineyards.[19] Probably due to the high quality of their wine, the Yuan government exempted Xunmalin from the usual tax on winemaking.[20]

It is possible that Xunmalin was not under the direct control of the Mongol khans. In 1229, the year he became the great khan, Ogodei already had an officially run textiles workshop under the charge of another Mongol commander, Zhenhai, who had also fought in the Khwarazmshah campaign. Zhenhai began by recruiting young boys and girls from many locales to settle in Hongzhou in modern Shanxi Province. He then obtained three hundred households of skilled golden silk textile weavers from "the Western Region" (most likely a reference to the Transoxiana region) to teach the young apprentices. Although this workshop produced textiles exclusively for the government, Ogodei granted the on-site management of the silk workshop to Zhenhai and his descendants.[21]

Even earlier, another colony of silk weavers had been settled within the Mongol empire, in Xinjiang. These weavers were immigrants from Herat, a city in western Afghanistan near the Iranian border that was famous for its weaving of gold brocade. Like Samarkand, it had been a part of the Khwarazmshah Empire. After conquering Herat in 1221, Mongol nobles moved many silk weavers eastward and settled them in Besh Baliq, northwest of the Xinjiang capital, Urumuqi. A decade or so later, Ogodei ordered a small portion of the population sent back to Herat to help rebuild that city. Those who remained at Besh Baliq continued to make excellent nasij for the great khan as well as the princes and princesses.

Soon after Khubilai became great khan in 1257, he established his capital at Dadu (modern Beijing). In 1276, a new bureau was established among the already numerous government offices in charge of textile production: the Bieshi Bali Ju, or Bureau of Besh Baliq, which was in charge of weaving a kind of "collar and sleeve nasij," according to the official Yuan Dynasty history.[22] The name suggests that the bureau was in charge of producing gold brocade especially for hemming collars and sleeves in the style of the Islamic tiraz borders. Eleven years later in 1287, a certain Zhama Lading, or possibly Jama al-Din, escorted to Dadu a group of weavers who specialized in a textile called Sadalaqi, and thereafter a Bureau of Sadalaqi was formed, using the staff of an earlier Bureau of Silk Yarn Processing.[23] Sadalaqi is most likely the Chinese transliteration of Zandaniji, Bukhara's most famous silk product. This was by no means the first time Zandaniji silks had arrived at a Mongol capital. Some seventy years earlier, they could be found in the inventory of the three Bukhara traders who had visited Genghis Khan in 1217 or 1218. What was different in 1287 was that Jama al-Din and possibly some others in his group were running a Bureau of Zandaniji in the Mongol capital in China and producing Zandaniji-style textiles, most likely with artisans transported from Bukhara.

With the abundant supply of high-quality silk fiber in China, Siberian gold that came from the forests just north of the Mongolian steppe, and skilled craftsmen from what had been the lands of Khwarazmshah, the Yuan Empire produced the best golden silk brocade in all of Eurasia. The production of gold brocade was the first priority of the Yuan government's huge bureaucratic system. To support this production, a Bureau of Gold Thread, Jinsizi Ju, was also created under the Administration of Official Workshops, which was in charge of making all the precious goods that required gold, jade, ivory, pearls, and silk.[24] By this time, the nasij made in Yuan China most likely had surpassed in quality that made in contemporary Iran and Transoxiana, the lands where it had first been developed. The production of gold brocade continued in Iran and Afghanistan under the Il Khanate, but no administrative records of this production have survived.

Although the gold brocades and other exquisite silks functioned essentially as the Yuan emperors' treasury, they did not intend to limit the wearing of such textiles to the royal family. They meant to make the entire empire take on a golden glow. The emperors granted expensive silk robes not only to their courtiers and commanders but also to the 12,000-strong imperial guards. According to Marco Polo, Khubilai Khan gave each of his 12,000 "barons" thirteen sets of silk robes, all of them garnished with gems and pearls. He wanted the imperial guards to have a different-colored robe for each month of the year.[25] The Yuan calendar might occasionally have a thirteen-month year. Though Marco Polo sometimes tended to exaggerate, this statement rings true. The Mongol tradition of clothing imperial guards in a way that would distinguish them from the regular army continued in China all the way through the Qing Dynasty, which did not fall until 1911. From the point of view of Khubilai Khan, dressing his imperial guards in such splendid uniforms was probably one of the most important ways he could demonstrate his own wealth and authority.

Dadu, the capital of the Yuan Empire, was never a tent city but a capital with well-built permanent structures. The imperial palaces, especially the dwelling of the Mongol emperor, were very much in the traditional Chinese architectural style. This agricultural and industrial setting was also a good place to produce the most exquisite textiles, not only silk, but also woolen textiles such as rugs and felt for tents.

Apparently, the gold silk mounted on felt, a suitable style for the tent palace on the Mongolian steppe, was not deemed sufficiently imperial-looking among the huge palatial buildings of Dadu. Thus Khubilai chose to display the imperial glory of his realm by dressing his entire retinue, including the palace guards, in gold brocade.

The Mongol rulers who remained on the steppe, living in the nomadic way, also needed gold brocade and other exquisite textiles, but they could not produce them. Despite the title of great khan, Khubilai Khan actually had very little, if any, control over his cousins who ruled the other three khanates. The Yuan Empire and the Il Khanate of Iran maintained a friendly relationship and frequently exchanged ambassadors and advisors. The other two regimes, the Chaghadai Khanate that controlled Central Asia and the Golden Horde on the Russian steppe, were often at odds with each other, the Il Khanate, and the Yuan Empire. The thoroughfares used by traders since the early centuries of the Common Era were hardly used at all in this period. In 1286, Khubilai Khan sent Bolad, a trusted prime minister, to the Il Khanate along with Isa, a Syrian, who served as his companion and interpreter. On their way back to China, via Central Asia, they encountered a rebellion and became separated. While Isa managed to return to Dadu after two hard years on the road, Bolad finally gave up on getting back to China and ended up staying in the Il Khanate to serve the Tuluid house of Mongol royals.[26]

Even so, some Muslim traders, with extensive geographical knowledge and language skills, did manage to travel westward through the vast area of steppe and oases, between the land of farming and the Mongol camps on the Chipchak steppe, bringing gold brocade to this far-off "Western Region." In the 1330s, the Moroccan traveler Ibn Battuta, during his first trip around Africa-Eurasia, witnessed the splendid cart procession of Muhammad Uzbeg Khan, the Mongol ruler of the Golden Horde. All the four *khatuns*, or queens of the khan, and their hundreds of attendants wore gold brocade and other fancy silk robes and scarves decorated with jewels. Even the horses pulling the carts were covered with gold silks.[27] The Mongols of the Golden Horde were frequently in contact with Constantinople, and one of the kahn's queens, Bayanlun, was the daughter of Andronicus III, the ruling emperor of Byzantium.

Through such contacts, commercial information about the east reached the Mediterranean world and even western Europe, where the gold brocade nasij was known as Tartar cloth.[28] This sort of commercial information lured the Polos and other Venetian merchants to undertake great risks in order to reach Mongolian-ruled China by the land routes. In the vast Mongol domains, Muslim officials, good or bad, maintained the bureaucratic systems and collected revenues for the Khanates, and traders sometimes still managed to obtain the much-desired silk textiles for both emperors and khans.

Beginning in the middle of the thirteenth century, the Mongol regimes that ruled over agricultural lands introduced the tent culture's upholstered furnishings, including both rugs and hanging tapestries, into interior décor. To make their palace halls in Dadu and Tabriz (the capital of the Il Khanate) resemble their tent homes on the steppe, Mongol emperors and nobles had woolen and silk rugs made to cover the floors and tapestries woven to hang on the walls. Rugs and tapestries became high fashion for ruling elites from the Pacific to the Atlantic, and forever changed the style of room decoration throughout Eurasia.

The Mongol conquest of southern China below the Yangzi River and the establishment of a sedentary empire throughout China also brought the Mongols into direct contact with overseas countries. During the fifty-year-long process of conquering south China, the Mongol army had learned the skills of navigation, or at least managed to recruit skilled sailors from the defeated Song army to build up a large naval force. Khubilai Khan used his newly acquired navy in an effort to invade Japan and Java but failed miserably in both places. The Yuan Empire never became a formidable sea power. However, the emperors became aware of the profits to be made from the growing seafaring trade. Many foreign traders came into the ports on China's southeast coast to trade, and some even settled there. Many of the latter were Muslim traders from western Asia. The Mongol rulers had long been familiar with this community of merchants and readily hired them as ortogs to carry out the trade with peoples living in the Southeast Asian archipelagos and to sustain long-standing connections with the Indian Ocean commercial networks.

Soon after the Mongol forces had secured China's southeastern coast, Khubilai assigned officials to collect tariffs on goods coming from overseas. He followed the Song custom of charging one-tenth of the value for luxury goods and one-fifteenth for staple goods. In 1277, formal customs offices were established in Quanzhou, Shanghai, Qingyuan (near modern Ningpo), and Ganpu (near modern Hangzhou). The customs officers were in charge of guiding the ships in and out of the harbors and arranging an annual gathering of sea traders to carry out the overseas commercial exchanges.[29] The port cities, especially Quanzhou, became home to merchants of many nationalities and religious affiliations. More than half of them were Muslims from Arab countries, such

When nomadic Mongols became Muslims around the fourteenth century, they erected tent mosques where they read the Koran. The upholsteries of tent culture—rugs, hangings, and folding racks for books—became popular in settled Eurasian communities as well. Bildarchiv Perussischer Kulturbesitz / Art Resource, NY

as Iran and Transoxiana, but Buddhist, Hindu, Christian, and Manichaean merchants also took up residence. Quanzhou became the key port linking Korean and Japanese traders to the networks of Southeast Asia. In Quanzhou they traded the bulk of their timber, ginseng, and musk for the spices, incense, and traditional medicines that came from the more southern, tropical lands.

By this time, silk was only one of many goods that China exported to the world, and tea and porcelain had become China's most numerous exports. During Yuan times, a white porcelain with designs and scenes painted on it in a cobalt blue pigment was famous throughout Eurasia, as well as the ports of East Africa, and brought in a large amount of revenue for the Yuan government. Large amounts of fragile porcelain ware had to be well packed in heavy, bulky wooden boxes, and it just was not feasible for caravans of horses or camels to carry these boxes across deserts or along steep mountain trails. The seafaring trade, however, could handle this cargo safely. Shiploads of porcelain set out from Quanzhou headed for Borneo, the Swahili coast of east Africa, Quilon on India's southwestern coast, and Siraf in the Persian Gulf. The sea routes at first overshadowed and then replaced the Eurasian land routes.

In the 1330s, famines and floods devastated the people of China, and the Mongol forces within China and on the steppe were too busy fighting among themselves to address the damage. Such conditions brewed rebellions, and in 1368, one of the rebel leaders defeated the Yuan and successfully established a new Chinese empire, the Ming. With the Mongols retreating back to the steppe, the production of nasij all but ceased, and eventually the other three khanates disintegrated as well. The caravan towns and religious facilities in Central Asia that had depended on the overland traffic declined. Abandoned, many of them were gradually covered by desert sands and disappeared from the landscape forever.

Chronology

ca. 250 BCE–226 CE
Parthian Empire rules Persia

221 BCE
Qin Dynasty unites China

206 BCE–220 CE
Han Dynasty rules China

Second century BCE to second century CE
Petra flourishes as caravan city

ca. 145 BCE
Sima Qian, the grand historian of China, born; Greek authority in Ai Khanoum, Afghanistan, ends

140–87 BCE
Reign of Han emperor Wudi

129 BCE
Zhang Qian reaches the court of the Yuezhi on the bank of the Oxus River

ca. 130 BCE–300 CE
Kushan Empire rules Afghanistan and extends its territory to India and part of Central Asia

100–200 BCE
Cyzicus travels to India via the Red Sea

Late second and early first centuries BCE
Parthians and Romans vie for Syria

104 BCE
General Li Guangli sets off to conquer Dawan so as to obtain its superior horses

64 BCE
The Parthians defeat the Seleucid regime

33 BCE
Han emperor Yuandi makes peace with the southern Xiongnu and sends Wang Zhaojun from his palace in Chang'an to be the bride of the chief Huhanxie

30 BCE
Egypt becomes a Roman province after the death of Cleopatra, the Ptolemaic queen

ca. 23–79 CE
Pliny the Elder lives

ca. 50
Kushans cross the Hindu Kush Mountains to enter India

Mid-first century
Periplus of the Red Sea in use as a manual for sailors

First century
Buddhism starts to spread out of India via Afghanistan

76
The Later Han emperor Zhangdi summons all military commanders to return to China from the Central Asian frontier; Ban Chao decides to remain on frontier

97
Gan Ying, sent by Ban Chao, travels to the coast of the "West Sea"—either the Persian Gulf or the Mediterranean—but does not reach Rome

First to second centuries
Parthia and India trade with the Romans "at sea"

148
Buddhist preacher An Shigao settles in Luoyang

165
The Romans take over Dura, conferring the name Europus on the city

227
Sassanid Dynasty replaces Parthian rule in southern Mesopotamia

256
Destruction of Dura, a caravan and garrison city

267
Odaenathus, king of Palmyra, successfully pushes back the invasion of the Sassanids

269
Palmyraean army occupies Egypt and a large part of Anatolia; Zenobia declares Palmyra independent from Rome

272–274
Roman emperor Aurelian sends Roman troops to suppress the rebellion in Palmyra

Later third and early fourth century
Kharoshthi script used in Niya, an oasis in the Takla Makan Desert

Fourth to fifth century
Development of the Bamiyan Buddhist complex

366
Creation of the Mogao caves in Dunhuang initiated

399–416
Faxian, accompanied by several monks, travels to India and returns to China

420
Xianbei conquers other petty states of nomadic origin and establishes the Northern Wei Dynasty

460
Northern Wei emperor initiates creation of huge statues of the Buddha at Yungang

527–565
Justinian I rules

532–537
Byzantine emperor Justinian I builds St. Sophia

589
Sui Dynasty unifies China

Early sixth century
The Turks appear on the northern border of China

571
The Turks commission Sogdian chief Maniakh as their ambassador to Byzantium

630
Xuanzang sets off for India from China

650–705
Reign of Empress Wu Zetian of the Tang Dynasty

651
Arabs conquer Iran

661–750
Umayyad Caliphate establishes the first Islamic empire, based in Damascus

704
Arab army starts conquest of Central Asia

750–1258
Abbasid Caliphate rules from Baghdad

751
Islamic army battles with Tang army at Talas, Central Asia

786–809
Caliph Harun al-Rashid rules

825–912
Ibn Khordadhbeh, Islamic geographer, lives

ca. 895
Byzantine emperor Leo VI issues *The Book of the Eparch* to the eparch (mayor) of Constantinople

969
Bishop Liudprand of Cremona visits Byzantium as an envoy of Otto I of Germany

1055
Seljuk Turks enter Baghdad and control the Abbasid Caliphate

1206
Genghis Khan (b. 1162) is proclaimed ruler of all the Mongols

1271
Khubilai declares himself the Chinese emperor of the Yuan Dynasty

1275–1292
Marco Polo travels in China

Notes

CHAPTER 1

1. Sima Qian, *Shi Ji* (Beijing: Zhonghua Shuju, 1959), 43/1808.
2. Sima Qian, *Shi Ji*, 43/1806–11.
3. Guan Zhong (?–645 BCE), *Guanzi* [Essays by Guan Zhong] (Beijing: Yanshan Chubanshe, 1995), 476, my translation.
4. Sima Qian, *Shi Ji*, 110/2883; 129/3260.
5. Sima Qian, *Shi Ji*, 110/2890.
6. Sima Qian, *Shi Ji*, 123/3158–59.
7. Sima Qian, *Shi Ji*, 123/3162, 3166.
8. Sima Qian, *Shi Ji*, 123/3168.
9. Chen Zhi, *Juyan Hanjian Yanjiu* [Studies on the Han wooden slips from Juyan] (Tianjin: Tianjin Guji Chubanshe, 1986), 492.
10. Lin Meicun, *The Western Regions of the Han–Tang Dynasties and the Chinese Civilization* (Beijing: Wenwu Chubanshe, 1998), 256–64.
11. E. Zürcher, "Han Buddhism and the Western Region," in *Thought and Law in Qin and Han China*, ed. W. L. Idema and E. Zürcher (New York: Brill, 1990), 158–82.
12. Note by Zhang Shoujie, a Tang Dynasty scholar, in Sima Qian, *Shi Ji*, 123/3162.
13. Victor Sarianidi, *The Golden Hoard of Bactria* (New York: Abrams, 1985).
14. Sima Qian, *Shi Ji*, 123/3174–77.
15. Ban Gu, *Hanshu* (Beijing: Zhonghua Shuju, 1964), 96a/3895.

CHAPTER 2

1. Pliny (23–79 CE), *Natural History,* trans. H. Rackam, vol. VI (London: Heinemann, 1961), xx.53–xxi.56.
2. M. Rostovtzeff, *The Social and Economic History of the Hellenistic World* (Oxford: Clarendon Press, 1941), 455–59.
3. Richard W. Bulliet, *The Camel and the Wheel* (New York: Columbia University Press, 1990), 216–36.
4. George Fadlo Hourani, *Arab Seafaring in the Indian Ocean in Ancient and Early Medieval Times* (Beirut: Khayats, 1963), 87–92.
5. M. Rostovtzeff, *Caravan Cities*, trans. D. and T. Talbot Rice (Oxford: Clarendon Press, 1932), 37–53.
6. Rostovtzeff, *Caravan Cities*, 50.
7. Gary Young, *Rome's Eastern Trade, International Commerce and Imperial Policy,* especially chap. 4, "The Trade of Palmyra" (London: Routledge, 2001), 136–86.
8. Rostovtzeff, *Caravan Cities*, chap. 5, "The Ruins of Palmyra," 120–52.
9. Andreas Schmidt-Colinet, Annemarie Stauffer, and Khaled Al-As'ad, *Die Textilien aus Palmyra* (Mainz: Verlag Philipp von Zabern, 2000).
10. Schmidt-Colinet, Stauffer and Al-As'ad, *Die Textilien aus Palmyra*, K240.

11. Rostovtzeff, *Caravan Cities*, 144.

12. Maurice Sartre, *The Middle East under Rome*, trans. Catherine Porter and Elizabeth Rawlings (Cambridge, Mass.: Harvard University Press, 2005), 357.

13. Rostovtzeff, *Caravan Cities*, 194–95.

14. Fan Ye (398–445), *Hou Han Shu* [History of the Latter Han] (Beijing: Zhonghua Shuju, 1965), 88/2919.

15. Strabo (ca. 63 BCE–24 CE), *The Geography of Strabo,* trans. Horace Leonard Jones (London: Heinemann, 1960), II.3.4.

16. Strabo, *Geography of Strabo*, II.5.12.

17. *The Periplus Maris Erythraei*, ed. and trans. Lionel Casson (Princeton, N.J.: Princeton University Press, 1989), 87. This English translation is better than the earlier *The Periplus of the Erythraean Sea*, trans. and annot. Wilfred Schoff (New York: Longmans, Green, 1912).

18. Casson, *The Periplus Maris Erythraei*, 65.

19. Casson, *The Periplus Maris Erythraei*, 51–53.

20. Casson, *The Periplus Maris Erythraei*, 61.

21. Casson, *The Periplus Maris Erythraei*, 63.

22. Casson, *The Periplus Maris Erythraei*, 67–69.

23. Casson, *The Periplus Maris Erythraei*, 67.

24. R. L. Bowen and F. P. Albright, eds., *Archaeological Discoveries in South Arabia* (Baltimore: Johns Hopkins University Press, 1958).

25. Casson, *The Periplus Maris Erythraei*, 67.

26. Casson, *The Periplus Maris Erythraei*, 73.

27. Casson, *The Periplus Maris Erythraei*, 77.

28. Casson, *The Periplus Maris Erythraei*, 79–81.

29. Casson, *The Periplus Maris Erythraei*, 78–79.

30. Casson, *The Periplus Maris Erythraei*, 81.

31. Casson, *The Periplus Maris Erythraei*, 87–89.

32. *Śilappadikāram*, trans. V. R. Ramachandra Dikshitar (Madras: Oxford University Press, 1939), 110.

CHAPTER 3

1. *Dialogues of the Buddha*, trans. T. W. and C. A. F. Rhys Davis (Oxford: Oxford University Press, 1921), iii 188.

2. Paul Bernard et al., *Fouilles d'Ai-Khanoum, Memoires de la Deligation archeologique Française en Afghanistan*, vols. 21, 22 (Paris: Editions Klincksieck, 1973).

3. Sima Qian, *Shi Ji* (Beijing: Zhonghua Shuju, 1959), 123/3164.

4. Gerard Fussman, "The Mat *Devakula*: A New Approach to its Understanding," in *Mathura: The Cultural Heritage*, ed. Doris Meth Srivasan (New Delhi: Manohal, 1989), 193–99.

5. Joseph Hackin, *Recherches archeologiques à Begram, chantier no. 2 (1937)* (Paris: Les Editions d'art et d'histoire, 1939); Hackin, *Nouvelles recherches archeologiques à Begram ancienne Kapici, 1939–40* (Paris: Imprimérie Nationale, Presses Universitaires, 1954).

6. John Marshall, *Taxila*, vol. 2 (Cambridge: Cambridge University Press, 1951), 406.

7. F. R. Allchin, "Evidence of Early Distillation at Shaikhan Dheri," in *South Asian Archaeology*, ed. Maurizio Taddei, Seminario di Studi Asiatici, Series Minor vi (Naples: Instituto Universitario Orientale, 1977), 755–97.

8. *The Saddharma-pundarīka* [The Lotus of the True Law], trans. H. Kern (Delhi: Motilal Banarsidass, 1980), 50–51.

9. Xinru Liu, *Ancient India and Ancient China, Trade and Religious Exchanges AD 1–600* (Delhi: Oxford University Press, 1988), chap. 4, "Buddhist Ideology and the Commercial Ethos in Kushan India," 88–102.

10. Liu, *Ancient India and Ancient China*, 92–102.

11. *The Larger Sukhāvatī-vyūha*, or *Description of Sukhāvatī, the Land of Bliss*, trans. F. Max Müller. vol. 49 (Delhi: Motilal Banarsidass, 1978), 33–34.

12. John Marshall, *Taxila*, vol. 1 (Cambridge: Cambridge University Press, 1951), chap. 10, and chap.11, "The Dharmajika," 231–95.

13. J. C. Harle, *The Art and Architecture of the Indian Subcontinent* (New Haven, Conn.: Yale University Press, 1994), chap. 2, "Early Rock-cut Architecture," 43–57.

14. Many of those inscriptions can be found in Jas Burgess, *Report on the Buddhist Cave Temples and their Inscriptions*, vol. 4 of *Archaeological Survey of Western India* (India: Bhartiya, 1975). A summary of the inscriptions can be found in Liu, *Ancient India and Ancient China*, 124–27.

15. Warwick Ball, "How Far Did Buddhism Spread West?" *Al-Rafidan* [Journal of Western Asiatic Studies] 10 (1989): 1–11.

16. Richard Salomon, *Ancient Buddhist Scrolls from Gandhara* (Seattle: University of Washington Press, 1999).

17. Thomas Burrow, *A Translation of the Kharoshthi Documents from Chinese Turkestan* (London: Royal Asiatic Society, 1940), 84–85, 95.

18. Huijiao (sixth century CE), *Gao Seng Zhuan* [Biographies of Outstanding Buddhist Monks], ed. and annot. Tang Yongtong (Beijing: Zhonghua Shuju, 1992), 4–12.

CHAPTER 4

1. Kalidasa, *Kumarasambhara* [The birth of Kumara], in *Works of Kalidasa*, ed. and trans. C. R. Devadhar, vol. 2 (Delhi: Motila Banarsidass 1984), vii.3.

2. Xuanzang, *Da Tang Xiyu Ji Jiaozhu* [Travel to the West during the Tang Dynasty], ed. Ji Xianli et al. (Beijing: Zhonghua Shuju, 1985), 130–31. *Chi*: a unit of measure equaling approximately one foot.

3. Xinru Liu, *Ancient India and Ancient China, Trade and Religious Exchanges AD 1–600* (Delhi: Oxford University Press, 1988), 151.

4. Alexander Kossolapov and Boris Marshak, *Murals Along the Silk Road* (St. Petersburg: Formica, 1999), 53–54.

5. Annette L. Julliano and Judith A. Lerner, eds., *Monks and Merchants: Silk Road Treasures from Northwest China* (New York: Abrams, 2001), 49.

6. Karl Jettmar, "Sogdians in the Indus Valley," in *Histoire et Cultes de L'Asie Centrale Préislamique*, ed. Paul Bernard and Frantz Grenet (Paris: Éditions du CNRS, 1991), 251–53.

7. B. I. Marshak and Valentina I. Raspopova, "Wall Paintings from a House with a Granary, Panjikent, 1st Quarter of the Eight Century A.D," in *Silk Road Art and Archaeology, Journal of the Institute of Silk Road Studies* 1 (1990): 123–75.

8. Marshak and Raspopova, "Wall Paintings," fig. 19, p. 146.

9. Xinru Liu, *Silk and Religion: An Exploration of Material Life and Thought of People, AD 600–1200* (Delhi: Oxford University Press, 1996), 73–79.

10. R. S. Lopez, "Silk Industry in the Byzantine Empire," *Speculum* 20 (1945): 1–43, 32.

11. Pliny's description of silk weaving in the Roman Empire ("and so supply our women with the double task of unraveling the threads and weaving them together again"), as quoted at the beginning of chapter 2, is not clear about why Roman

women had to unravel the threads. But an encyclopedia of Chinese institutions, the *Tong Dian*, compiled in Tang China by Du You (735–812) says that the Romans unravel plain Chinese textiles to make exquisite silk textiles. Du You, *Tong Dian* (Beijing: Zhonghua Shuju, 1988), 193/5265.

12. Meyer Reinhold, *The History of Purple as a Status Symbol in Antiquity* (Brussels: Latomus, 1970), 70.

13. Xinru Liu, "Silk, Robes, and Relations between Early Chinese Dynasties and Nomads beyond the Great Wall," in *Robes and Honor: The Medieval World of Investiture*, ed. Stewart Gordon (New York: Palgrave, 2001), 23–34, 31.

14. Liu, *Ancient India and Ancient China, Trade and Religious Exchanges*, 51.

15. As related by the mid-sixth-century author Yang Xuanzhi, *Luoyang Qielan Ji* [Memories of holy places in Luoyang], ed. Fan Xiangyong (Shanghai: Guji Chubanshe, 1978), 2.

16. Loyang Archaeological Team of the Institute of Archaeology, Chinese Academy of Science, "Excavation of the Tower-base at the Yong-ning Temple of Northern Wei Dynasty," *Kaogu* [Archaeology] 3 (1981): 223–34, 212.

17. Phyllis Ackerman, "Textiles through the Sasanian Period," in *A Survey of Persian Art*, ed. Arthur Uphan Pope, vol. 2 (New York: Maxwell Aley Literary Associates, 1981), 693, 681–715.

18. Procopius, *The Anecdota or Secret History*, trans. H. B. Dewing (London: Heinemann, 1928), xxv.22–25.

19. Étienne de la Vaissière, *Sogdian Traders: A History* (Leiden: Brill, 2005), 209, 228, 233–35.

20. D. C. Shepherd and W. B. Henning, "Zandaniji Identified?" in *Aus der welt de islamischen kunst* (Berlin: Festschrift Ernst Kühnel, 1959), 15–44.

21. D. C. Shepherd, "Zandaniji Revisited," in *Documenta Textilia*, ed. M. Fleury-Lemberg and Karen Stolleis (Munich, 1981), 105–22.

22. Yang Xuanzhi, *Luoyang Qielan Ji*, 329.

CHAPTER 5

1. Wang Han, *Liangzhou Ci*, in Shen Zufen, *Tangren Qijueshi Qianshi* [Annotations of Qijue poems of Tang Poets] (Shanghai: Guji Chubanshe, 1981), 11. My translation.

2. Xinru Liu, *Silk and Religion: An Exploration of Material Life and the Thought of People, AD 600–1200* (Delhi: Oxford University Press, 1996), 188–89.

3. Related by the late seventh- and early eighth-century author Zhang Cu, *Chaoye Jianzai* [Anecdotes inside and outside the Tang Court], ed. Zhao Shouyan (Beijing: Zhonghua Shuju, 1979), 148.

4. Related by the seventh-century authors Huili and Yanzong, *Da Ci'en Si Sanzangfashi Zhuan* [Biography of Hsuanzang the Dharma Teacher of Ci'en Monastery], ed. Sun Yutang and Xie Fang (Beijing: Zhonghua Shuju, 1983), 160.

5. Liu, *Silk and Religion*, 70–72.

6. Liudprand, *The Works of Liudprand of Cremona*, trans. F. A. Wright, chap. 54 (London: Routledge, 1930), 268.

7. Meyer Reinhold, *History of Purple as a Status Symbol in Antiquity* (Brussels: Latomus, 1970), 70.

8. Mas'udi, *The Meadows of Gold*, trans. and ed. Paul Lunde and Caroline Stone (London: Kegan Paul, 1989), 24–25.

9. Liu, *Silk and Religion*, 136–37.

10. Bernard Lewis, *Islam: From the Prophet Muhammad to the Capture of Constantinople* (New York: Oxford University Press, 1987), 140–41.

11. Mas'udi, *Meadows of Gold*, 390.
12. Mas'udi, *Meadows of Gold*, 390.
13. Mas'udi, *Meadows of Gold*, 239.
14. Nicolas Oikomonides, "Silk Trade and Production in Byzantium from the Sixth to the Ninth Century: The Seals of Kommerkiarior," Dumbarton Oaks Papers, vol. 11 (Washington, D.C.: Dumbarton Oaks Research Library and Collection, 1986), 41–47.
15. Du Huan, *Jingxing Ji* [Travelogue], ed. Zhang Yi (Beijing: Zhonghua Shuju, 2000), 52.
16. *The Book of the Eparch*, 239–40.
17. Ibn Khordâdhbeh (825–912), *Kitâb al-Masâlik Wa'l-Mamâlik*, trans. into Chinese by Song Xian as *Daoli Bangguo Zhi* [Records of roads and countries] (Beijing: Zhonghua Shuju, 1991), 116.

CHAPTER 6

1. Rashīd al-Dīn, *Jāmi' al-tavārīkh*, vol. 1 (Tehran: Eqbal, 1959), 439, quoted in Thomas Allsen, *Commodity and Exchange in the Mongol Empire: A Cultural History of Islamic Textiles* (Cambridge: Cambridge University Press, 1997), 12.
2. Ata-Malik Juvaini, *Genghis Khan: The History of the World-Conqueror*, trans. and ed. J. A. Boyle (Seattle: University of Washington Press, 1997), 77–78.
3. Juvaini, *Genghis Khan*, 79.
4. Thomas Allsen, "Mongolian Princes and Their Merchant Partners, 1200–1260," in *Asia Major*, 3rd ser., vol. 3, pt. 2 (Princeton, N.J.: Princeton University Press, 1989), 89, 83–154.
5. Yelü Chucai, *Xiyou Lu* [Journey to the West], 1. My translation.
6. Yelü Chucai, *Xiyou Lu*, 2–3. My translation.
7. Yelü Chucai, *Xiyou Lu*, 2–3. My translation.
8. Juvaini, *Genghis Khan*, 120.
9. Juvaini, *Genghis Khan*, 122.
10. Translator's introduction to Juvaini, *Genghis Khan*, 27–29.
11. Song Lian et al., *Yuanshi* [History of the Yuan Dynasty] (1370) (Beijing: Zhonghua Shuju, 1976), 3063–70.
12. Henry Yule and Henri Cordier, eds., *The Book of Ser Marco Polo*, vol. 1 (Delhi: Munshiram Manoharlal, 1993), 415; Song Lian et al., *Yuanshi* 250/4558–64.
13. Allsen, "Mongolian Princes and Their Merchant Partners, 1200–1260," 85, nn. 8, 9.
14. Allsen, "Mongolian Princes and Their Merchant Partners, 1200–1260," 98–99.
15. Juvaini, *Genghis Khan*, 21–22.
16. Allsen, "Mongolian Princes and Their Merchant Partners, 1200–1260," 96.
17. Juvaini, *Genghis Khan*, 237.
18. Juvaini, *Genghis Khan*, 238–39.
19. Song Lian et al., *Yuanshi*, 122/3016; Rashid al-Din (ca. 1247–1318), *The Successors of Genghis Khan*, trans. John Andrew Doyle (New York: Columbia University Press, 1971), 276, quoted in Allsen, *Commodity and Exchange in the Mongol Empire*, 42.
20. Song Lian et al., *Yuanshi*, 19/419.
21. Song Lian et al., *Yuanshi*, 120/2964.
22. Song Lian et al., *Yuanshi*, 85/2149; Thomas Allsen, *Commodity and Exchange in the Mongol Empire*, 40–41.
23. Song Lian et al., *Yuanshi*, 85/2149.

24. Song Lian et al., *Yuanshi*, 88/2225–27.

25. Yule and Cordier, *Book of Ser Marco Polo*, vol. 1, 394.

26. Thomas Allsen, *Culture and Conquest in Mongol Eurasia* (Cambridge: Cambridge University Press, 2001), 72.

27. Ma Jinpeng (translated into Chinese), *Yiben Baitutai Youji* [Itinerary of Ibn Battuta] (Yinchuan: Nixia Renmin Chubanshe, 1985), 271.

28. Allsen, *Commodity and Exchange in the Mongol Empire*, 1–4.

29. Song Lian et al., *Yuanshi*, 94/2401.

Further Reading

GENERAL WORKS

Beckwith, Christopher I. *Empires of the Silk Road: A History of Central Eurasia from the Bronze Age to the Present*. Princeton, N.J.: Princeton University Press, 2009.

Bregel, Yuri, ed. *An Historical Atlas of Central Asia*. Boston: Brill, 2003.

Cribb, Joe and Georgina Herrmann, eds. *After Alexander: Central Asia before Islam*. New York: Oxford University Press, 2007.

Foltz, Richard C. *Religions of the Silk Road: Overland Trade and Cultural Exchange from Antiquity to the Fifteenth Century*. New York: St. Martin's Press, 1999.

Whitfield, Susan. *Life along the Silk Road*. Berkeley: University of California Press, 1999.

CHAPTER 1

Barfield, Thomas. *The Perilous Frontier: Nomadic Empires and China, 221 BC to AD 1757*. Cambridge, Mass.: Blackwell, 1989.

Hopkirk, Peter. *Foreign Devils on the Silk Road*. London: Murray, 1980.

Khazanov, Anatoly, and André Wink, eds. *Nomads in the Sedentary World*. London: Curzon Press, 2001.

Sima, Qian. *Records of the Grand Historian*. Translated by Burton Watson. Rev. ed. New York: Columbia University Press, 1993.

———. *The First Emperor: Selections from the Historical Records*. Translated by Raymond Dawson. Oxford: Oxford University Press, 2007.

Yu, Yingshi. *Trade and Expansion in Han China*. Berkeley: University of California Press, 1967.

CHAPTER 2

Bowen, Richard L., and Frank P. Albright. *Archaeological Discoveries in South Arabia*. Baltimore: Johns Hopkins University Press, 1958.

Groom, Nigel. *Frankincense and Myrrh: A Study of the Arabian Incense Trade*. London: Longman, 1981.

The Periplus Maris Erythaei. Translated by Lionel Casson. Princeton, N.J.: Princeton University Press, 1989.

The Periplus of the Erythraean Sea. Translated and annotated by Wilfred Schoff. New York: Longmans, Green, 1912.

Rostovtzeff, M. *Caravan Cities*. Translated by D. and T. Talbot Rice. 1932. Reprint, New York: AMS Press, 1971.

Sartre, Maurice. *The Middle East under Rome*. Translated by Catherine Porter and Elizabeth Rawlings. Cambridge, Mass.: Harvard University Press, 2005.

Young, Gary K. *Rome's Eastern Trade, International Commerce and Imperial Policy 31 BC–AD 305*. London: Routledge, 2001.

CHAPTER 3

Benjamin, Craig G. R. *The Yuezhi: Origin, Migration and the Conquest of Northern Bactria*. Turnhout, Belgium: Brepols, 2007.

Hawkes, Jason, and Akira Shimada, eds. *Buddhist Stupas in South Asia*. Delhi: Oxford University Press, 2009.

Liu, Xinru. *Ancient India and Ancient China: Trade and Religious Exchanges AD 1–600* Delhi: Oxford University Press, 1988.

Marshall, John Hubert. *Taxila: An Illustrated Account of Archaeological Excavations Carried Out at Taxila under the Orders of the Government of India between the Years 1913 and 1934*. Cambridge: Cambridge University Press, 1951.

Ray, Himanshu. *Monastery and Guild: Commerce under the Satavahanas*. Delhi: Oxford University Press, 1986.

Zürcher, E. *The Buddhist Conquest of China: The Spread and Adaptation of Buddhism in Early Medieval China*. 3rd ed. Leiden: Brill, 2007.

CHAPTER 4

Juliano, Annette L., and Judith A. Lerner, eds. *Monks and Merchants: Silk Road Treasures from Northwest China*. New York: Abrams, 2001.

Marshak, Boris. *Legends, Tales, and Fables in the Art of Sogdiana*. New York: Bibliotheca Persica Press, 2002.

La Vaissière, Etienne de. *Sogdian Traders: A History*. Translated by James Ward. Leiden: Brill, 2005.

Liu, Xinru. *Silk and Religion: An Exploration of Material Life and the Thought of People, AD 600–1200*. Delhi: Oxford University Press, 1996.

CHAPTER 5

Constable, Olivia Remie. *Housing the Stranger in the Mediterranean World: Lodging, Trade, and Travel in Late Antiquity and the Middle Ages*. Cambridge: Cambridge University Press, 2006.

Gordon, Stewart. *Robes and Honor: The Medieval World of Investiture*. New York: Palgrave, 2001.

Hodgson, Marshall G. S. *The Venture of Islam*. Vols. 1–2. Chicago: University of Chicago Press, 1974.

Sen, Tansen. *Buddhism, Diplomacy, and Trade: The Realignment of Sino-Indian Relations, 600–1400*. Honolulu: University of Hawai'i Press, 2003.

Silverstein, Adam J. *Postal Systems in the Pre-modern Islamic World*. Cambridge: Cambridge University Press, 2007.

CHAPTER 6

Allsen, Thomas. *Commodity and Exchange in the Mongol Empire: A Cultural History of Islamic Textiles*. New York: Cambridge University Press, 1997.

———. *Culture and Conquest in Mongol Eurasia*. New York: Cambridge University Press, 2001.

Komroff, Manuel, ed. *The Travels of Marco Polo*. New York: Liveright, 2003.

Websites

About Japan
http://aboutjapan.japansociety.org/
   Includes thirty essays on varied topics
   from Japanese history and society, all
   by recognized scholars; also includes
   teaching resources.

Buddhist Art and Trade Routes
www.asiasocietymuseum.com/
buddhist_trade/index.html
   Images, maps, and articles about
   Buddhist art and the Silk Road,
   provided by the Asia Society.

China: Dawn of a Golden Age
www.metmuseum.org/special/China/
index.asp
   Online exhibit at the Metropolitan
   Museum of Art, featuring short
   articles and images of sculptures and
   artifacts from the Silk Road, as well
   as a glossary, chronology, maps, and
   suggested reading.

**Cleveland Museum of Art Indian and
Southeast Asian Collection**
www.clevelandart.org/explore/
department.asp?deptgroup=11&
   More than 1,000 images of Indian
   and Southeast Asian art and artifacts,
   searchable by keyword, date, and
   medium.

Dunhuang Academy
www.dha.ac.cn/
   Photos and information on the history
   of selected grottos from the Mogao
   caves.

Heilbrunn Timeline of Art History
www.metmuseum.org/toah/
   The Metropolitan Museum of Art
   provides timelines and articles on art
   from all over the world, divided into
   regions. The sections on Asia and the
   Iberian and Italian peninsulas are most
   relevant for students of the Silk Road.

Hermitage Museum
www.hermitagemuseum.org/
   Many of the collection highlights
   displayed in the "Oriental Art" section
   relate to the Silk Road.

**International Dunhuang Project:
The Silk Road Online**
http://idp.bl.uk/
   An international collaboration of
   institutes holding the world's best
   Silk Road collections. Includes a
   searchable database of art, artifacts,
   and documents; articles and
   newsletters on Silk Road history and
   research; and a categorized list of links
   to useful sites.

Kyoto National Museum Gallery
www.k-gallery.net/
   Displays images of archaeology,
   ceramics, sculpture, Buddhist painting,
   ink painting, sutras and scriptures,
   calligraphy, textiles, lacquer ware,
   metalwork, architecture, and historical
   documents. Search by country, time
   period, or keyword. The collection
   covers China, Korea, and Japan,
   1000 BCE–1800 CE.

**Monks and Merchants: Silk Road
Treasures from Northwestern China,
Gansu and Ningxia**
http://sites.asiasociety.org/arts/
monksandmerchants/
   Online exhibit from the Asia Society
   presenting images of sculptures,
   artifacts, and documents, each with a
   short article.

Palace Museum
http://newweb.dpm.org.cn/
shtml/2/@/8797.html
   The Palace Museum of the
   Forbidden City in Beijing provides
   virtual exhibits and a selection of

"Curator's Picks" of the treasures and architecture of the Ming and Qing dynasties.

Silk Road Seattle
http://depts.washington.edu/silkroad/index.html

A public education project sponsored by the University of Washington, this sprawling web site includes illustrated articles on history, architecture, and culture; annotated bibliographies; an electronic atlas; and historic documents translated into English.

Topkapi Palace Museum
www.ee.bilkent.edu.tr/~history/topkapi.html

Illustrated articles on the history, architecture, and treasures of the Topkapi Palace in Istanbul.

Acknowledgments

This book was commissioned by the Oxford University Press eight years ago as part of a project to interpret world history for a new generation of students and general readers. To make the complex and exciting subject comprehensible for this audience, I enlisted help from colleagues and friends. Professor Thomas Allsen, a scholar of world history from the College of New Jersey, did critical editing of the entire text. Chapter 6, on the Mongol Empire, draws heavily from his scholarship. Professor Denise Spellberg, a specialist on Islamic history from the University of Texas at Austin, read the first two chapters and offered her critique on the writing. A young friend, Rebecca Fraimow, squeezed out hours from her tight high school senior year schedule to read and edit the text. My friend and mentor of world history Professor Lynda Shaffer helped me edit and revise the entire book. I extend my gratitude to all of them, while taking responsibility for any remaining mistakes.

Index

Page numbers in **bold** indicates maps or illustrations.

fragrances, 98
frankincense, 23–24, 35, 37, 39, 55
furs, 4, 38, 98, 118

Gan Ying, 18, 128
Gandhara
    artworks, 79
    Buddhism, 52, 55
    Kushan Empire, 39, 46, 50
    Northern Wei Dynasty, **63**, 85
    Sanskrit, 58
Ganfu, 6–7
Ganges River, 40, **56**, 85
Ganpu, 124
Gao Xianzhi, 101
Gaochang, 90, 113
Gate of Jade, 9–13
gemstones, 10, 66, 79, 101, 122
Genghis Khan, 109, 111–22, 129
geographers, 34, 129
Germanic tribes, 62, 75, 92
Ghanzi, 105
Ghaznavids, 105
glassware, 10, 35
Gnostics, 69
Gobi Desert, **2**
gold
    aureus coin, 47
    gold thread, 37, 74, 102, **103**, 118–19,
        122
    Kushan Empire, 17
    maritime trade, 35
    Seven Treasures, 54
    Siberia, 122
    Yuezhi, 3
Golden Horde, 117, 123
Grand Colonnade, 28
The Great Mongol Shahnama, **119**
Great Wall
    construction of, 4
    extended to Gate of Jade, 9–12
    military garrisons, 9–10, 11–12
    Mongol Empire, 120–21
    nomad migrations, 76
    Qin Dynasty, **2**, 4
    silk trade, 82
    Tang Dynasty, 87
    Zhang Jun burial goods, **9**
Greece
    Ai Khanoum, **2**, 44–45
    Alexander the Great, 7, 33, 44
    architectural influences of, **25**, 26, 27, 28,
        31, 44–45, 49

and Bactria, 40, 44
coinage, 40, 47, **48**
frankincense and myrrh, 23
Kushan Empire, 43, 46
language of trade, 27, 29
maritime trade, 34
Nabataeans and, 27
olive oil, 29
and Palmyra, 28, **30**, 31
Periplus of the Red Sea, 34–41
Petra, 28
Ptolemies, 21
viticulture, 29
Guanzi, 3
guilds, 102
Gulf of Cambay, 36, 39, 41
Gupta Empire. *See* India

Hadith, 94
Hadrian, 31
Hagia Sophia, 73
Haidari, 57
Han Dynasty
    blood-sweating horses, 17
    brocades, 10, 15, **16**
    Buddhism, 60–61
    burials, 15
    Confucianism, 77
    decline of, 87
    dowries, 4–5
    embroidery, 10
    emergence of, 4–5, 127
    horses, 12, 17–18
    maritime trade, 33
    naming conventions, 60
    and nomads, **2**, 62, 75
    oasis states, 20
    *Official History of the Former Han
        Dynasty*, 18
    Palmyra burials, 28, **30**
    Parthian Empire, 18–19, 61
    passports, 12
    and the Romans, 18–19
    silk trade, 31
    taxation, 10
    transitions of, 14
    woolen textiles, 10, 18
    Wudi, 127
    Xiongnu, **2**, 4–5, 8–9, **9**, 18, 21
Harun al-Rashid, 98
Hasanna, 120
Hephthalites, 64, 84–85
Herat, **110**, 121

Kaaba, 94, **95**
Kalidasa, 62
Kalyana, 55
Kanishka, 47, **48**, 61
Kapisi, 48, **56**
kapok, 20
Karakorum, **110**, 111, 115, 117, 119
Kashmir, 30, 38
Kezil, 64, 65
Kharoshthi, 128
Kharoshthi script, 46–47, 58–59
Khasneh, **25**, 26
Khorasan, 115
Khordâdhbeh. Ibn, 102, 129
Khotan, 3, 14, 59, **63**, **110**, 113
Khubilai Khan, 116, 122–24
Khurasan, 38
Khusro, 81, 82
Khwarazmshah Empire, 112–16, 121
Kommerkiarior, 100
Koran, **125**
Korea, 125
Kucha, **63**, 64–65
Kushan Empire
    Afghanistan, 15, 46, 48, 127
    agriculture, 79
    artworks, 17, 49–50
    Bactria, 45, 85
    bronze scale weight, **45**
    Buddhism, 42, 50–51
    burials, 17
    and China, 61
    and coinage, 43, 47, **48**
    cosmopolitanism, 42–43, 47–48, 50
    established, **2**, 15
    fall of, 62, 67
    gemstones, 38
    gold, 17
    and Greece, 43, 46
    Gupta Dynasty, 63
    Hinduism, 43
    horses, 17, 44, 49
    invade India, 38, 127
    ivory, 17
    Jainism, 43
    Kharoshthi script, 46–47, 58–59
    Lotus Sutra, 79
    maritime trade, 48
    Mathura, 39, 46–47, **56**
    nomads, 43
    Persian Empire, 43, 46
    precious stones, 38
    Roman Empire, 41, 47

Sassanid invasion, 58, 63
    and the Silk Road, 38, 42, 48
    taxation, 43, 45, 47
    Western Pure Land Sutra, 79
    and the Yuezhi, 79
    Zhang Qian, 45

lacquer ware, 48, 113–14
lapis lazuli, 38, 54, 67
Leo VI, 92, 129
Levant, 22
Li family, 87
Li Guangli, 18, 127
Li Xian, 80
Liao Empire, 110–11
linen, 30
Liu, Xinru, 133n14
Liudprand, 92, 129
Longmen, 78
Lotus Sutra, 52–53, 79
Loulan, **16**, 18
Luo, 4
Luoyang, 60, **63**, 67, 78–79, 128

Mahayana Buddhism. *See* Buddhism
Mahmud Khwarazmi, 112
Maijishan, 65
Malik Shah, 105
Maniakh, 82, 129
Manichaeism, 60, 66, 69. *See also* religions
maps, **2**, **21**, **56**, **63**, **70–71**, **110**
maritime trade
    Africa, 36
    Arabia, **21**, 36–37
    Arabian Sea, 34, 41, **56**
    Barbaricum, 38–41, **56**
    Barygaza, 38–40, 55, **56**
    vs. camels, 108
    Cape of Spices, 36
    decline of the Silk Road, 109, 126
    emergence of, 108
    Greece, 34
    Han Dynasty, 33
    vs. horses, 108
    Indian Ocean, **2**
    Kushan Empire, 48
    Mongol Empire, 124–26
    Nabataeans, 36
    navigation, 22–23, 34–41, 124–26, 128
    Nile River, 34, 35
    Palmyra, 31
    Parthian Empire, 33
    porcelain, 108, 109, 110, 126

Xinru Liu (Ph.D. University of
Pennsylvania) teaches early Indian
history and world history at the College
of New Jersey. She is associated with
the Institute of History and the Institute
of World History, Chinese Academy
of Social Sciences. She is the author
of *Ancient India and Ancient China:
Trade and Religious Exchanges, AD
1–600* (1988); *Silk and Religion: An
Exploration of Material Life and the
Thought of People, AD 600–1200*
(1996); *Connections across Eurasia:
Transportation, Communication, and
Cultural Exchange on the Silk Roads*,
co-authored with Lynda Norene Shaffer
(2007); and *A Social History of Ancient
India* (1990 in Chinese). She is one
of the authors of the world history
textbook *Worlds Together, Worlds
Apart.*

The
New
Oxford
World
History

CHRONOLOGICAL VOLUMES
The World from 4000 to 1000 BCE
The World from 1000 BCE to 300/500 CE
The World from 300 to 1000 CE
The World from 1000 to 1500
The World from 1450 to 1700
The World in the Eighteenth Century
The World in the Nineteenth Century
The World in the Twentieth Century

THEMATIC AND TOPICAL VOLUMES
The City: A World History
Democracy: A World History
Empires: A World History
The Family: A World History
Race: A World History
Technology: A World History

GEOGRAPHICAL VOLUMES
Central Asia in World History
China in World History
Japan in World History
Russia in World History
The Silk Road in World History
South Africa in World History
South Asia in World History
Southeast Asia in World History
Trans-Saharan Africa in World History